ALL-PRO BASEBALL STARS 1981

Bruce Weber

D1372346

SCHOLASTIC BOOK SERVICES

New York Toronto London Auckland Sydney Tokyo

**To the Schalls and their
descendants, who we found
many years too late**

Material for *All-Pro Baseball Stars 1981* closed on
December 20, 1980

The Author would like to express thanks to the American and
National League public relations offices and the major-league
team publicists for their help in assembling the material for this
book.

Cover photo: Focus on Sports

ISBN 0-590-31989-2

12 11 10 9 8 7 6 5 4 3 2 1   3   1 2 3 4 5 6/8

Printed in the U. S. A.   06

CONTENTS

American League All-Pro Team 1980

1B:	Cecil Cooper
2B:	Willie Randolph
SS:	Robin Yount
3B:	George Brett
OF:	Willie Wilson
OF:	Ben Oglivie
OF:	Reggie Jackson
C:	Rick Cerone
RHP:	Steve Stone
LHP:	Tommy John

← Cecil Cooper will be counted on heavily to lead Brewers to the American League pennant.

1

First Base
CECIL COOPER
MILWAUKEE BREWERS

Brother, did Cecil Cooper ever pick the wrong year to hit .352. The 31-year-old's 1980 mark was good enough to win an American League batting crown in any year — except the one in which George Brett hit .390.

This one-time Boston Red Socker with the odd batting stance creamed the ball from start to finish last season, with three hitting streaks of 15 or more games. He hit safely in four out of every five Brewer outings. And he became the first Brewer ever to get more than 200 hits in a season. (He had 219.)

Was Cecil upset about being ignored last summer? Nope. "I can't take anything away from George. He really did it. It's not bad to hit .352 and finish second when the other guy hits .390 to beat you. I know that if I keep getting the numbers, people are going to hear about me."

Teammate Sal Bando, one of the Brewers' dynamic leaders, marvels at Cooper. "I've played with some guys who've had great seasons. But none of them had the all-around year like Cecil had last year. He can really use the bat. Imagine, 122 RBI's, 25 homers, even 17 steals. He could swipe 30 bases a year if he wanted to. And he's a master in the field. He can do it all."

The 6'2", 190-pounder is a natural. He's a fine hitter because he uses the whole field. George Brett knows he'd better keep at least one eye on Cecil Cooper.

Second Base
WILLIE RANDOLPH
NEW YORK YANKEES

In the Yankee game-plan, Reggie Jackson and Bob Watson are the big bats. They knock in the runs. But that requires men on base, and that's where Willie Randolph fits in. The slim second sacker was on base nearly 43% of the time last year, second best in the AL. And so the Yankees won 103 games, best in the majors. The Yankee game-plan works.

Good defense and a high on-base percentage. That's Willie's game. Few American League second basemen handle a glove or make the double play quite like the 25-year-old Randolph. He is blessed with great range in the field and a fine arm.

At the plate, Willie's 119 walks was the top mark for a Yankee since Mickey Mantle received 122 free passes back in 1962. Randolph's total included at least one walk in each of the Yanks' last 15 games, when the Eastern Division title was on the line.

Willie got off to a terrible start in 1980, sliding to .128 two weeks into the season. But he bounced back to hit .294 for the year. He also stole 30 bases, which was tops on the club.

"I was pressing too hard when the season began," remembers Randolph. "I thought if I didn't get on base, I'd be hurting the team. So, naturally, I didn't get on base. When I finally got my act together, learned to hold back and relax at the plate, everything was fine."

New Yankee manager Gene Michael hopes that everything stays fine for his All-Star second baseman.

ROBIN YOUNT
MILWAUKEE BREWERS

It's hard to remember when anyone but Robin Yount was the Brewers' shortstop. The solid six-foot, 170-pounder has owned the position for seven years. And he won't be 26 years old until next September.

Like another Robin, Batman's partner, this boy wonder picked up his 1000th big-league hit last August. The 1000-hit circle isn't very select. But Yount reached it a month before his 25th birthday. In that respect, he joined Hall of Famers like Al Kaline and Ty Cobb. That's good company.

Ex-Brewer manager George Bamberger is one of Yount's biggest fans. "He takes success well," says Bamberger. "He's completely unselfish and he gives you 100% every game. He never lets up."

Last season was a typical Yount year. The Illinois native played in 143 games, banged 179 hits — including 23 homers, knocked in 87 runs, and stole 20 bases. Milwaukee fans have come to expect that kind of production from the American League's top shortstop.

"If Robin stays healthy," says Bamberger, "there's no telling how good he can be. Remember, he never got any minor-league training. It probably took him a little longer to get ready in the majors. But he's rolling now. I can see him playing shortstop in Milwaukee for another fifteen years."

By that time, Robin could easily have 3,000 or more hits. And that is a select circle.

GEORGE BRETT
KANSAS CITY ROYALS

The baseball story of 1980? It's not even close. It was George Brett's near-miss with the magic .400 batting average. George's face graced the cover of every magazine. His voice was heard on every newscast. Students, office workers, and housewives everywhere discussed his nightly performances over countless lunches everywhere.

George didn't make it, of course. He ended up hitting only .390. He was victimized by an injury-riddled season. Nonetheless, his mark was the highest in the majors since Ted Williams' .406 in 1941. Will 1981 be George's year? Maybe.

George Brett, a solidly built, six-foot, 200-pounder, is just about the prettiest-looking hitter in baseball. He has the kind of stroke the real fans love to watch. (Only California's Rod Carew is in the same class.) Besides his batting mark, Brett led the AL in slugging (.664) and on-base percentage (.461). And despite missing nine games with a bruised heel in May, 26 games with a torn ankle ligament in June and July, and then nine more with tendinitis in his right hand in September, he still hit a career-high 24 homers, knocked in 118 runs, smacked nine triples, and had 296 total bases.

Do Kaycee rivals respect George? You bet! Baltimore's Earl Weaver once walked him to load the bases (first base wasn't open). The Oriole pitcher then walked in the winning run. The Yankees won't soon forget his giant three-run homer that won the third and final AL playoff game. And despite painful minor surgery during the World Series, George still managed to hit .375 in the loss to Philly.

Outfield
WILLIE WILSON
KANSAS CITY ROYALS

What's faster than a speeding bullet? It's either Superman or Willie Wilson. And the fans in Kaycee will pick their man of steal over the Man of Steel any day.

The Royals' 25-year-old left fielder blossomed in 1980, establishing himself as one of the young greats in the game. Despite a disastrous World Series, Willie enjoyed a fabulous year at bat, on the bases, and in the field. Check these numbers: tops in the American League in at bats (705, an all-time big-league record), hits (230), runs (133), and triples (tied with 15). He had the second-highest steals mark (79), the seventh best batting average (.326), and the ninth best total bases figure (297).

That kind of performance raised the former New Jersey high school star's career bat mark to .307. And his all-time record for stolen bases (216 for 254) gives him a stunning 85% success rate.

The 6'3", 190-pounder, a one-time high school football All-American, was headed for the U. of Maryland before the Royals' money halted his college plans. It was one of Kaycee's all-time best moves. Speed-demon Willie, who's always a threat to steal, tied Pete Rose's big-league record for hits by a switch-hitter. His 32 straight stolen bases between July 20th and September 30th smashed Ron LeFlore's old AL record (27).

Tough at bat, flashy in the field, and greased lightning on the bases...Willie will lead the Royals' championship outfield for the next ten years!

BEN OGLIVIE
MILWAUKEE BREWERS

The Brewers' new manager, Bob Rodgers, shoots straight from the hip. "Ben Oglivie," he says, "is the best left fielder in baseball. He's quick, he has great baseball instincts, and he has super range. He's the best." End of commercial.

Rodgers slept a little better over the winter knowing that Gentle Ben would be patrolling the outfield for his Milwaukee team this summer. Lefty Oglivie does pretty well at the plate too. Though his friend and teammate, Cecil Cooper, over-shadowed him with the bat, Ben's numbers weren't too shabby: a .304 average, 180 hits, a league-leading (with Reggie Jackson) 41 homers, and 118 RBIs.

At 6'2" and only 170 pounds, Oglivie's build can only be described as wiry. He can hide in the shadow of Milwaukee's other slugger, 6'3", 200-pound Gorman Thomas. Ben's 41 homers thus seem even more incredible.

"I'm a line-drive man," says Ben. "I can't explain the home runs either. I go up to the plate, just to make contact and hit the ball hard. All of a sudden, it's going out. And I seem to be hitting left-handers as well as rightys."

Rodgers thinks he knows the secret of Oglivie's success. "He has great wrists," says the Brewers' boss. "With his compact swing, he's a legitimate home run threat."

Oglivie, whose off-the-field interests include music and philosophy, is delighted. "I'm playing every day (156 games last year). That's the best news of all."

13

Outfield
REGGIE JACKSON
NEW YORK YANKEES

If Mr. October had done a little better in August and September, he might have won his second American League Most Valuable Player award. As it was, 1980 was just fine, thank you, for Reginald Martinez Jackson, the most talked about player in baseball.

The 34-year-old had his first .300 season ever at bat, smacked 41 homers (his second-best figure and tied for the AL lead), and drove in 111 runs. By hitting 25 or more four-baggers for the 10th straight year, he approaches a select circle of all-timers who did it for 11 or more years. The others? Babe Ruth, Willie Mays, Jimmy Foxx, Lou Gehrig, and Eddie Matthews. Not bad.

The candy-bar man started 1980 like a steamroller. By mid-season, he looked like a shoo-in for the MVP. But, as George Brett got hot and closed in on .400, Jackson slumped. He recovered in time to key the Yankees' late pennant drive, smashing the clinching homer against Detroit on the next-to-last day of the campaign.

The six-foot, 206-pound Jackson is probably as smart as he says he is. Nonetheless, the Philadelphia native has a unique ability to get involved in all sorts of problems. This off-season it was a demand for money, lots of it. While Yankee boss George Steinbrenner tried to sign free-agent Dave Winfield, Reggie announced that he expected some reward, too—like a million dollars a year for the next five years.

Catcher
RICK CERONE
NEW YORK YANKEES

Life is beautiful for 26-year-old Rick Cerone. When the Yankees plucked him off the Toronto Blue Jays' roster to replace the late Thurman Munson, Rick knew he'd be playing a high-pressure role.

But the New York area native was more than up to it. A lifetime .228 hitter coming in, Rick got off to a slow start at the plate, then caught fire. He raised his average from .202 in mid-May to finish at .277, easily his best year ever. His 85 RBIs were second to Jackson among the Yanks and topped his total for the two previous years combined.

There was never any question about Cerone's defensive ability. The durable 5'11", 185-pounder tossed out nearly half of the enemy runners who tried to steal against him. No other catcher in the American League came close.

Rick has been successful at just about every kind of athletic activity. In high school (New Jersey's Essex Catholic), he threw 13 TD passes in his senior year for the undefeated football team. He also starred in baseball and, would you believe, fencing. At Seton Hall U., he was a two-time All-American catcher, setting nearly every bat mark in the school's record book.

But nothing could match the kind of performance he gave in his first year back home—with the Yankees. A great year at the bat, an even better year behind the plate, and a divisional title.

STEVE STONE
BALTIMORE ORIOLES

How do you turn a pitcher with a less than .500 career record and a lifetime 4.24 earned run average into a Cy Young Award winner? Steve Stone, the Oriole right-hander who pulled off that nearly impossible trick, doesn't really know for sure. If he did, he could bottle and sell it.

The 33-year-old from Cleveland wandered from team to team (the Giants, White Sox, Cubs, and Sox again) before landing in Baltimore as a 1979 free agent.

That was Stone's big break. "I got some great advice from pitching coach Ray Miller," Stone recalls. "He told me to cut down my time between pitches. And he advised me to forget about using all five of my pitches during the early stages of a game. That really helped. I'll never have another losing season."

Big talk, but Stone's 1980 performance backs it up. Steve's 25-7 record led the majors in wins. Though he lost two of his first three decisions, he recovered to win 14 in a row (from May 9th to July 26th) and 19 out of 20.

"I guess I just got tired of losing," says Stone. "After I hurt my arm in 1976 (a torn rotator cuff), I worked hard to strengthen it. It helped my fastball. My curve was always pretty good. Now I start getting myself mentally ready a couple of days before I'm going to pitch. It works!"

Pitcher
TOMMY JOHN
NEW YORK YANKEES

20

The Yankees' ace lefty (sorry about that, Ron Guidry fans) continues to amaze the doctors and New York opponents. In the fifth, full season following his first-of-a-kind elbow surgery, the "Bionic Arm" turned in his second straight 20-win season in his second Yankee campaign.

Matter of fact, Tommy John is the winningest pitcher in the game over the last two seasons, with 43 victories and only 18 losses. His 22-9 performance in 1980 was a major factor in the Yanks' Eastern Division title. Though his earned run average slipped to 3.43, John's worst since 1971 (with the White Sox), he remains the best example of the value of hard work.

Tommy, who'll be 38 on May 22nd, wears his age well. There's no overpowering fastball in his bag of tricks. Instead, there's one of the most effective sinkers in the game, as well as a sharp curve and a sneaky-fast fastball. When Tommy is hot, the batters take mighty swings at his slow stuff and wind up banging the ball into the ground. He works the corners like a traffic cop, usually forcing the batters to go after a pitch that's down and away.

Retirement? Forget it. Tommy isn't even thinking about it. "My body may be 38 years old," he says, "but my arm is only six years old. There are a lot more pitches in it."

National League
All-Pro Team
1980

1B: **Steve Garvey**
2B: **Manny Trillo**
SS: **Garry Templeton**
3B: **Mike Schmidt**
OF: **Dusty Baker**
OF: **Jose Cruz**
OF: **George Hendrick**
C: **Gary Carter**
RHP: **Jim Bibby**
LHP: **Steve Carlton**

Steve "Lefty" Carlton of the world-champ Phillies doesn't talk to the press. But he "talks" to Phils' opponents every time he goes to the mound. His 24-9 record, 2.34 ERA, and 286 strikeouts won him the 1980 CY Young Award.

First Base
STEVE GARVEY
LOS ANGELES DODGERS

Last summer wasn't the happiest for Dodger leader Steve Garvey. The famous story in a national magazine which revealed problems in Garvey's home life shocked many fans and deeply upset Steve and Cyndy Garvey. They sued the publisher. It wasn't pretty.

But did Steve's game suffer? The veteran's performance says no.

Steve hit .304, seventh in the league. And he smashed 200 hits, tops in the NL. That marked Steve's sixth 200-hit season in the last seven years. Few players in history can point to that kind of year-in, year-out record.

One more record attests to Garvey's status as the NL's top first-sacker. It's his durability. Steve played in all 163 Dodger games in 1980. That shouldn't come as a surprise. Garvey has now played in 835 straight games and 1,125 of the last 1,134. Though Lou Gehrig's all-time iron-man feat of 2,130 games in a row is only a dream, Steve could make it. The bad news is that he'll have to stay healthy and productive until the last day of the 1988 season—when he'll be 39 years old. Pete Rose can tell Steve that anything is possible.

Steve doesn't worry about consecutive-game marks. (He thinks that Billy Williams' National League record, 1,117 straight, is a more realistic goal than the Gehrig mark.) But his major target every year is 300-200-100. That means a .300 bat mark, 200 hits, and 100 RBIs. Steve hasn't missed since 1977. He believes that 1981 will be no exception.

Second Base
MANNY TRILLO
PHILADELPHIA PHILLIES

When you think of the Phillies, you think immediately of slugging Mike Schmidt, Pete "Charley Hustle" Rose, and "Lefty" Carlton. If you're like most fans, you forget the glue that holds the whole works together. That's second baseman Manny Trillo.

Manny blends into the background, doing his job well every day. Although a late-season slump banged his batting average down to .292 (from .337 in July), Manny did everything an All-Pro second baseman is supposed to do throughout the 1980 season.

Though the Mets' Doug Flynn prevented Manny from winning his second-straight Gold Glove Award, there's little doubt about Trillo's ability in the field. He's always among the NL leaders in double plays, thanks in part to his low, submarine delivery to first. Incoming runners find themselves bailing out early to prevent contact between ball and head.

Manny is slim, bordering on skinny. He's 6'1" and weighs only 160 pounds. The heat of summer and the long season are bound to take their toll on the native of Venezuela, who started his pro career as the world's thinnest catcher. The shift to second came during his first tour of duty in the Phillies' farm system. Later he was dealt to Oakland—where Charley O. Finley tried to sneak him on to the A's roster for the 1973 World Series. After another stop with the Cubs, Manny came back to Philly — to stay. He's now in the second year of a five-season, $2.1 million-dollar contract. And he's worth every penny.

Shortstop

GARRY TEMPLETON

ST. LOUIS CARDINALS

28

Is Garry Templeton for real? Not everyone is convinced yet. But he has come far enough to put plenty of space between himself and the rest of the National League shortstops. (Dave Concepcion fans please note your hero's .260 batting average and Templeton's .319.)

Cardinal fans are certain that Garry's injuries, which kept him out of 44 St. Louis games, was a key factor in the Redbirds' slow 1980 start. The Cards spent much of the early season in the NL East basement while Templeton healed.

Once he got back into the lineup, the rangy 5'11", 170-pounder did it all. In only 118 outings, he managed 161 hits, 43 RBIs, and 31 stolen bases on the way to his .319 hit mark. He joined such heavy hitters as Keith Hernandez, Ken Oberkfell, Ted Simmons, and George Hendrick in pacing St. Louis to the National League's best team average — .275.

The switch-hitting 25-year-old is unique in that he's just as effective from either side of the plate. In 1979, he became the first switcher in baseball history to compile 100 or more hits from both sides. His quarter-season on the sidelines prevented a repeat of this enormous feat in 1980.

Garry's critics point to his defensive weaknesses in attempting to downgrade his talent. There's no question that his arm is a problem and some nifty fielding plays at first have saved him even more errors. But his speed and his bat make him the NL's best at short.

MIKE SCHMIDT
PHILADELPHIA PHILLIES

If Mike Schmidt could bottle the ingredients of his 1980 season, he could make a
fortune. Schmitty did it all for the Phils'

world champions. And his performance hardly went unrewarded. He won the daily double — the National League MVP Award (by a unanimous vote for only the second time in NL history) and the World Series MVP Trophy. That's the kind of season you put into a memory book, ready to refer to whenever things get tough.

Mike has been the Phillie third-sacker for eight years. His success rate has been tremendous. Four times he has been the NL's All-Star third baseman. He practically owns the Gold Glove award. But nothing matches 1980 for Mike. Check these numbers: a career high .286 batting average, 48 homers, the most ever by a third baseman, 121 RBIs, 342 total bases, and a .624 slugging percentage—all tops in the league.

Mike also turned in some of the greatest clutch hitting ever. He had 17 game-winning RBIs, including four in the last five Phils' wins, when the National League East title was on the line. He was just as good in the World Series, with a .381 bat mark, seven RBIs, and two round-trippers.

The secret of Schmidt's success? Mike says he played a little heavier last year. "I gained about twelve pounds," he says, "most of it through weight-lifting. I can't think of any better reason why I raised my batting average by thirty-three points."

Mike might make a ton of money by bottling his success formula. But he'll do just as well if he keeps playing as he did in '80.

DUSTY BAKER
LOS ANGELES DODGERS

The Dodgers made their best play of 1980 five weeks *after* the season ended.

Five minutes before Dusty Baker was to become a free agent, Los Angeles signed him to a new five-year contract.

The bottom line on Baker's new pact reads $4 million. Nobody will be running any benefits for the 6'2", 187-pounder who has been rooting for the Dodgers since his California childhood. Now, at age 31, Johnnie B. Baker, Jr., known much better as Dusty, becomes the highest-paid Dodger of all-time.

Signing Baker may have been the Dodgers' best move. But it can't rank much higher on the team's list than the trade which brought Dusty from Atlanta in time for the 1976 season. (The Braves had originally selected Dusty as a *25th round* draft choice in 1967.)

A lifetime .274 hitter coming into the 1980 campaign, Dusty had his best all-around season last year. He hit .294, knocked in 97 runs, and bombed 29 homers, which was the best among the Dodgers. He could be considered the least popular Dodger in New York, where he feasted on Met pitching all-year long.

An injury to Reggie Smith (he missed 70 games) thrust Baker into the Dodger spotlight in 1980. That helped him win headlines for the first time in his career. "I guess my lack of great press stems from the fact that I do a lot of things well, but nothing spectacularly," says Baker. "I don't mind — as long as we win."

Dusty is now doing one thing spectacularly well — making money. His "game" isn't far behind.

JOSE CRUZ
HOUSTON ASTROS

34

Is there a real baseball fan alive who can forget the scene of Jose Cruz sobbing uncontrollably after the Phils eliminated the Astros from the National League playoffs last fall? Of course not. Cruz's reaction wasn't surprising. Perhaps more than any other Astro, he kept the team's act together throughout the summer when the "experts" everywhere gave up on Houston.

The oldest (at age 33) of three baseball-playing Cruz brothers (Tommy and Hector are the other two), Jose put it all together in his tenth big-league season. He hit .302, 11th best in the National League. He played in 160 of Houston's 163 games (including the one-game playoff win over L.A.), led the team with 185 hits and 91 RBIs, and contributed 15 game-winning hits, sixth best in the league. Eleven homers and 36 stolen bases completed his fine offensive season.

Jose also proved himself on defense in 1980. Outfield lapses raised questions about his ability in '79. But Jose had his best year in the field last season, joining Cesar Cedeno and Terry Puhl in Houston's championship outfield. And the three did just well enough at the plate to help the Astros edge the Dodgers.

The Cardinals ought to be arrested for stealing. St. Louis sent San Diego pitcher Eric Rasmussen in 1978 and picked up George Hendrick. All Hendrick has done is hit .300 or better for two straight years and now adds an NL All-Pro outfield spot. (Rasmussen was 4-11 for the 1980 Padres.)

Like most of the Redbird hitters, George was at his best for the fourth-place finishers. (Their pitching was another story.) Three weeks before the end of the season, Hendrick was leading the league's hitters at .325. A late slump reduced his average to .302, tenth in the league, but still 27 points above his career mark.

The 6'3", 195-pounder knocked in 109 runs, second only to Mike Schmidt among National Leaguers, and 23 better than his previous all-time high. The figure is even more impressive when you remember that George hit fifth in the Cards' batting order most of the season.

Unlike Rodney Dangerfield, Hendrick gets lots of respect. When *The Sporting News* asked National League players to pick their All-Star right fielder, George's rivals gave him nearly five times as many votes as his closest rival, Phillie Bake McBride.

The 31-year-old Hendrick has spent some time with Oakland and Cleveland in addition to San Diego and St. Louis. But, with back-to-back .300 seasons, he seems to have found a home in Missouri—unless Whitey Herzog can use him to find a little of that pitching he needs so much.

GARY CARTER
MONTREAL EXPOS

When the Expos finished their 1980 season's business against the Phillies, their

All-Star catcher, Gary Carter, might have been the tiredest man on the field. As tired as he was, however, he would have preferred to do further business against the west champion Houston Astros and the American League kingpins, the Kansas City Royals.

The Expos' second-straight near-miss in the NL East was particularly disappointing to their 26-year-old backstop, who might very well be the best catcher in baseball. The disappointment stems from Gary's late-season charge at the bat which keyed the Expos' pennant drive. During September, Gary played in all 28 Expos' games, no mean feat for a catcher. Tired or not, Gary tagged the ball at a .360 clip, good enough to win him National League player-of-the-month honors. Gary was even better during an end-of-the-month, two-week Montreal road trip. With all the chips on the line, Carter hit in 12 of the 13 games (for a .429 bat mark), smacked five doubles, five homers, and knocked in 16 runs. That's doing it in the clutch.

For the season, the key numbers were .264, 29 homers, and 101 ribbies. That's a big year for anyone, especially one who catches most of his team's games.

Gary is looking for an improvement in his working conditions in 1981. "I don't want to catch 150 games again. It's a killer. I don't want to burn myself out. I've got to get some help behind the plate. And do I ever want to play in Canada's first World Series!"

JIM BIBBY
PITTSBURGH PIRATES

Jim Bibby offers perfect proof that life may well begin at 35. The football-sized (6'5", 250 pounds) Pirate right-hander had his best year ever in 1980, winning 19 and losing only six for the Bucs. His long, sizzling hot summer kept Pittsburgh in the National League East hunt until the last weeks of the season, when he and the team slumped.

The well-traveled Bibby spent eight years kicking around the Mets' farm system (including two years in the service and one on the disabled list with a back injury) before hitting the big-time with the St. Louis Cards in 1972. He enjoyed only one better-than-.500 season (13-7 with Cleveland in 1976) before arriving in Pittsburgh in 1978.

Bibby, the brother of pro basketball's Henry Bibby, actually believes that his delayed career may have contributed to his recent great success. "I think I'm stronger now than most guys my age because I missed three seasons," he says.

Though most players prefer fewer career stops than Bibby, he feels that he profited from his travels. "With the Texas Rangers, I learned plenty from Fergie Jenkins. With Cleveland, I was tutored by Harvey Haddix and Jeff Torborg."

Haddix, now with the Bucs, takes no credit for Bibby's tremendous improvement. "He has done it all by himself," says the man with the 12-inning perfect game. "He worked plenty hard perfecting his delivery. He used to be a fastball-only pitcher. He tried to overpower everyone. Now he can go to his curve in the clutch."

STEVE CARLTON
PHILADELPHIA PHILLIES

They call him "Lefty," just "Lefty." There are millions of left-handed people in Philadelphia, but just one "Lefty."

He's Steve Carlton and he is, simply, the best pitcher in baseball. Since he came to Philly from St. Louis (for Rick Wise) in 1972, he has been the big man, the stopper. Over the years, he has converted from an overpowering fastballer to a wise, crafty pitcher. He has added one of baseball's best sliders and a variety of other pitches to the still-effective fastball.

Lefty's new catcher, Bob Boone (Tim McCarver was once his regular backstop), marvels at Carlton. "You have to be strong to throw that slider and you have to believe in your ability to get it over the plate. Lefty has it all."

What Lefty doesn't have is a long list of newspaper interviews. Several years ago, he decided to go silent. And he has kept up the barrier of silence through good years and better. Last year he also decided to stuff his ears with cotton during games in order to drown out the crowd noise. It helps him concentrate.

Must be something to it. At age 35, Carlton unrolled a dynamite season in 1980. Manager Dallas Green handed him the ball 38 times; 13 times Steve was around at the finish. He won 24, lost only nine, and turned in an unbelievable 2.34 ERA in a whopping 304 innings with 286 strikeouts. With a healthy, effective Carlton, the Phils will always remain in the NL East hunt.

THE ROOKIES
AMERICAN LEAGUE

JOE CHARBONEAU
CLEVELAND INDIANS

Super Joe. That's what they call Joe Charboneau in Cleveland. And Joe is the first to agree.

"I know I can do it," says the 6'2", 200-pound outfielder. "If I hadn't gotten hurt late in the season, I would have hit .300. That's one of my goals for 1981."

His rookie year wasn't too poor. Joe hit .289 with 23 homers. The round-trip total would've been higher except that he played in only 131 games and was limited to 47 at-bats (mostly as a pinch-hitter) after September 1st. Indian doctors diagnosed his groin injury after the season and cleared it up with medicine.

"I'm glad they found out what it was," says Joe. "I was bothered by the problem for two straight years. Now I'm ready to roll."

Joe's rookie year wasn't all happy. He was stabbed during an anti-American demonstration in Mexico City in the spring. He went 1-for-31 during mid-July (and was benched for six games). And then came the injury. But Joe was clearly the No. 1 rookie in the American League.

Other AL Rookie stars: P Doug Corbett, Minnesota; 2B Damaso Garcia, Toronto; P Britt Burns, Chicago.

STEVE HOWE
LOS ANGELES DODGERS

Give the Dodgers credit. In Brooklyn and in Los Angeles, they've always come up with the great rookies. That's why the Dodgers are usually in the thick of the pennant race.

Now add lefty pitcher Steve Howe to the list that includes: Jackie Robinson, Don Newcombe, new San Diego manager Frank Howard, Rick Sutcliffe, and a host of others.

Steve deserved it. His work in Tom Lasorda's bullpen was brilliant. After only 13 games in the minors, he got his shot in the majors and did everything with it. He pitched in 59 games with a 2.65 earned run average. In 41 games, from May 6th through September 20th, he pitched 63 innings and allowed only seven earned runs. That's an incredible 1.00 ERA pace.

Going into 1980, Steve figured he had only an outside shot at making the Dodgers. But when the chance came—Don Stanhouse's injury—he was more than up to it.

Other NL Rookie stars: P Bill Gullickson, Montreal; OF Lonnie Smith, Philadelphia.

AMERICAN LEAGUE
1980 STANDINGS

East

	Won	Lost	Pct.	GB
New York	103	59	.636	—
Baltimore	100	62	.617	3
Milwaukee	86	76	.531	17
Boston	83	77	.5187	19
Detroit	84	78	.5185	19
Cleveland	79	81	.494	23
Toronto	67	95	.414	36

West

	Won	Lost	Pct.	GB
Kansas City	97	65	.599	—
Oakland	83	79	.512	14
Minnesota	77	84	.478	19½
Texas	76	85	.472	20½
Chicago	70	90	.438	26
California	65	95	.406	31
Seattle	59	103	.364	38

and Previews for 1981

AL East
NEW YORK YANKEES

Ho-hum! So the Yanks have a new manager. What else is new? New York fits into a pattern: the team wins, then fires the field boss. This time it's Gene Michael for Dick Howser.

Michael figures to win another AL East title for The Bronx. He's got the pitching, with 22-9 All-Pro Tommy John heading a superb cast of starters and 6'2" Goose Gossage (33 saves) the bullpen star. That's not all, of course. Ron Guidry (17-10) is still one of the premier lefties in the game.

The Yanks overcame a bunch of physical problems to win the east in '80. A healthy 3B Graig Nettles (.244) can still do the job. 2B Willie Randolph (.294) is the AL's best. Last year's free agent steal, 1B Bob Watson (.307) did exactly what was expected of him. SS Bucky Dent (.262) is, at least, consistent.

The outfield has defensive problems. CF Rupert Jones (.223) missed half the season. All-Pro Reggie Jackson (.300, 41 homers) made it with his bat, not his glove.

Second-best in the American League? That's not the Yanks' style. So George Steinbrenner opened the bank again last December, pulled out every moneybag in the vault, and came up with San Diego's Dave Winfield, now at $1.5 million or more per year, baseball's No. 1 money man.

Paul Molitor

AL East
MILWAUKEE BREWERS

The Brewers are trying to wipe out memories of last year's 17-games-behind, third-place AL East finish. They've got a new manager (Bob "Buck" Rodgers) and he likes his chances.

Milwaukee banged the ball at a .275 clip last year and figures to do even better this time around.

The newest big bat belongs to switch-hitting C Ted Simmons, the ex-Cardinal, who had 21 homers and 98 RBIs to go with his .303 average in '80. He joins All-Pros like 1B Cecil Cooper (.352, second only to George Brett), SS Robin Yount (.293), and LF Ben Oglivie (.304). The rest of the cast isn't shabby either. Gorman Thomas (.239) hit 38 homers and knocked in 105 runs. Paul Molitor hit .304 and, if Larry Hisle (.283) is healthy, the Brewers will have one of the most potent line-ups around.

Ex-Card Pete Vuckovich (12-9) and relief ace Rollie Fingers (11-9, 2.80, 23 saves for San Diego) join the mound staff. Fingers may be the Brewers' first real bullpen ace.

Simmons, Vuckovich, and Fingers cost the Brewers right-hander Larry Sorenson (12-10, 3.68), OF Sixto Lezcano (.229). and two very talented minor-leaguers. But for the immediate future, at least, the Brewers win this one.

Scott McGregor

AL East
BALTIMORE ORIOLES

The Orioles spent part of the off-season trying to charm Ron Shapiro. Maybe you never heard of him, but he was a key man in the Birds' 1981 planning.

Shapiro is a lawyer, a sports lawyer. Among his Baltimore clients: Eddie Murray, Ken Singleton, Scott McGregor, and Rich Dauer. Those four form the core of manager Earl Weaver's team.

1B Murray (.300) led Baltimore with 32 homers and 116 RBIs, both career highs. He's only the fifth switch-hitter in history to stroke 30 or more round-trippers. Switch-hitting OF Singleton (.304) cracked the .300 barrier for the fourth time and drove in 104 runs, topping 100 for the third time. 2B Dauer (.284) was the majors' toughest strike-out man (only 19 in 618 appearances). Catchers Rick Dempsey and Dan Graham had 24 homers and 94 RBIs between them. And Birds' MVP, OF Al Bumbry set club records for hits (205) and singles (158).

As usual, pitching is no problem in Baltimore. CY Young Award winner Steve Stone (25-7) was joined by Scott McGregor (20-8) who joined the 20-win circle on the final day. Underwear model Jim Palmer (16-10) still has it at 35, and lanky Tim Stoddard (5-3, 26 saves) leads the bullpen.

If the Yanks falter, the O's are ready.

Steve Kemp

AL East
DETROIT TIGERS

Manager Sparky Anderson has the Tigers on the verge of greatness. At most the team is a player, maybe two, away from the top. The 84-78 record in 1980 was no fluke.

The Tigers are blessed with solid hitting (.273) and pretty good pitching (4.25 ERA). And they've got what Ponce deLeon could never find — a fountain of (talented) youth.

SS Alan Trammell, just 23, excelled with a .300 bat mark and 65 RBIs. He could be the AL's shortstop of the future. Tom Brookens, off his first full season (.275), should improve.

Strongboy Steve Kemp (.293, 21 homers, 101 RBIs) provides outfield power. One-time Red Champ Summers (.297) could be a late-bloomer (he's 32 years old). Al Cowens (.268, but .280 after coming over from California) adds depth.

Lance Parrish (.286) and John Wockenfuss (.274) form an excellent catching team. But their pitchers are question marks. Righties Milt Wilcox (13-11) and Jack Morris (16-15) were the big winners among the 1980 starters. Aurelio Lopez (13-6, 21 saves) needs help in the Tiger bullpen. If Mark Fidrych (2-3) can come back or Dave Tobik, Roger Weaver, Jerry Ujdur, or ex-Padre Dennis Kinney can make it, the Detroit pitching will improve.

Jim Rice

AL East
BOSTON RED SOX

With "The Major," Ralph Houk, now in command, the Sox still have the same problems which have been driving their managers bananas for years. It's pitching; actually it's the lack of pitching.

Boston has always been blessed with great hitters. Big righty Steve Crawford, 2-0 with the Sox in September after coming up from Bristol (Eastern), is the latest new hope. But Houk will need more. The team's 4.38 ERA in 1980 was horrible.

Bullpen ace Tom Burgmeier is one of the Sox top performance (5-4, 2.00 ERA, 24 saves). Righty Bob Stanley (10-8, 3.39) can start or relieve. Mark Clear, the ex-Angel who arrived with IF Carney Lansford and OF Rick Miller, will help. Lefty John Tudor impressed with an 8-5 mark and a 3.02 ERA in 13 Boston starts.

The Sox can hit, of course, as their nifty .283 team average proves. Though SS Rick Burleson (.278) and 3B Butch Hobson are gone to California, 3B Glenn Hoffman (.285) and 2B Dave Stapleton (.321) had super rookie years.

C Carlton Fisk (.289) can still hit, though his days behind the plate are numbered. OF Jim Rice (.294, 86 RBIs, in only 124 games) is healthy again. OF Fred Lynn (.301 in only 110 games) was on the trading block.

Mike Hargrove

AL East
CLEVELAND INDIANS

When the 1980 season ended, the Indians knew they needed pitching. They might have gotten it from Pittsburgh. The new Indian on the reservation is righty Bert Blyleven, whose dismal 8-13 and 3.82 marks last year are mysteries Cleveland hopes to unravel.

The Pittsburgh-Cleveland deal also brought aging Manny Sanguillen, a crafty pinch-hitter, and cost the Tribe a couple of pitchers (2-9 Bob Owchinko and 6-7 Victor Cruz) and catcher Gary Alexander (.225). Advantage: Cleveland.

The Indians' 4.68 ERA was incredibly high. Even the big winners—Len Barker (19-12) and Dan Spillner (16-11)—owned awful ERAs (4.17 and 5.28 respectively). The trade leaves lefty Sid Monge (3-5, 14 saves) all alone in the bullpen.

To go 79-81 with that pitching staff, the Indians had to hit. And they did (.277). Rookie-of-the-Year Joe Charboneau (.289) led the club in homers (23) and RBIs (87). Switch-hitting LF Miguel Dilone, an early-season steal from the Cubs, hit .341 (.353 hitting lefty). 1B Mike Hargrove, ever consistent, hit .304 with 11 homers and 85 ribbies. Mid-season addition Alan Bannister hit .324 for Cleveland (and .281 overall). Former All-Pro Toby Harrah (.269) scored 100 runs.

Alfredo Griffin

AL East
TORONTO BLUE JAYS

The Jays continue to show improvement, though it's painfully slow. They should progress again in '81—and still slowly. (Toronto's .563 percentage last April—they went 9-7—marked their best month ever.)

The trade which sent Rick Cerone to the Yankees before last season created a hole behind the plate that hasn't been filled. Though Toronto drafted three free-agent catchers, they failed to sign one.

SS Alfredo Griffin (.254) is one of the hopefuls. He tied Willie Wilson for the major-league triples crown (15). 1B-DH John Mayberry (.248) stroked 30 homers. OF Otto Velez (.269) enjoyed a four-homer double-header. 2B Damaso Garcia broke in with a .278 year, including 30 doubles and 46 RBIs.

Pitching improved—with Dave Stieb (12-15) the best of the lot. The team's 4.19 ERA was .63 better than in '79. Lefty Jerry Garvin (4-7, 2.29 ERA, 8 saves) is solid in the bullpen. Ex-Met Roy Lee Jackson may help.

Toronto will be more respectable — but will remain in the East basement.

Rookies to watch: C Brian Miller, P Charlie Puleo.

Willie Aikens

KANSAS CITY ROYALS

There are always new worlds to conquer. On their fourth try, the Royals finally beat the Yankees to win the AL pennant. Now the World Series presents a challenge. The loss to the Phils probably served to strengthen Kaycee.

Though the Royals should repeat in the AL West, it's doubtful whether they can do it as easily as in 1980 when they breezed in by 14 games. But the ingredients are there.

3B George Brett may not hit .390 again, but he's too good a hitter to ever flop. All-pro Willie Wilson (.326, 79 steals) will bounce back from his horrible World Series swan-dive. Vet Hal McRae (.297) hit .386 during a 40-game stretch when Kaycee — sewed things up. The rest of the crowd — including 1B Willie Aikens (.278), CF Amos Otis (.253), 2B Frank White (.264), SS U. L. (Toothpick Man) Washington (.273) — is back, along with a bunch of young talent.

Pitching is more than good. Chief fireman Dan Quisenberry went 12-7 with 33 saves. Lefty Larry Gura (18-10) pitched 16 complete games with a 2.95 ERA. Steady Dennis Leonard had his third 20-win season (20-11). The staff ERA was a creditable 3.83 — plenty when the team *bats* .286 like the champs did!

Al Oliver

AL West
TEXAS RANGERS

It's out of the Boston frying pan for Don Zimmer — and into the Texas fire. (And we aren't just talking about last summer's heat wave.)

The chunky Zim, who won everything at Boston except the pennant, takes over a Texas club that should have done better than 76-85 (20½ games behind) under Pat Corrales a year ago.

Zimmer has some new faces, in part because of some Rangers' cost-cutting. Powerful Richie Zisk, (.290, 19 homers) big contract and all, is gone, along with four pitchers (most notably Ken Clay). They're all Seattle Mariners now. The new Texans include four players who may — or may not — help the Rangers move up: OF Leon Roberts (.251), C Larry Cox, P Rick Honeycutt (10-17), and SS Mario Mendoza (.245).

The Rangers can hit. Last year's team .284 average was the second-highest in baseball. Team MVP CF Mickey Rivers had a dynamite year (.333, 210 hits). Speedy OF Al Oliver (.319), solid 3B Buddy Bell (.329 former All-Pro C Jim Sundberg — (.273), and 2B Bump Wills (.263) form a solid core on offense.

Pitching is something else. Zimmer hopes Honeycutt and former Phillie Kevin Saucier (7-3) will help returnees like Doc Medich (14-11, but a 3.93 ERA) and lefty Jon Matlack ·

55

Matt Keough

AL West
OAKLAND A's

Now comes the moment of truth for Billy Martin and his amazing Oakland A's. The one-time AL West doormats rose to second place in 1980 and no one can figure out how manager-of-the-year Martin did it. But, of course, he did it well.

With Charles O. (former owner) Finley gone, the A's can concentrate on baseball all season. Problem is Martin usually starts running into trouble during his second year with every club. Should be interesting.

Martin has the same fine, young players he molded into an 83-79 winner. Super righty Mike Norris (22-9, 2.63 ERA) is back, along with 16-13 Matt Keough and 14-14 Steve McCatty. The team ERA was a nifty 3.46, best in the AL. Martin spent the off-season looking for a reliever.

The outfield is solid with Tony Armas (.279, 109 ribbies, 35 homers), Stolen-base King Rickey Henderson (.303), and Dwayne Murphy (.274). Mitchell Page, who sat out 52 games, is far better than his .244 average indicates.

Around the infield, Dave Revering's .290 mark included 11 game-winning hits in only 106 games. Switch-hitting Dave McKay hit .244 in 123 games, the most played by any Oakland infielder. If the A's have a weakness, it's in the infield.

AL West
CALIFORNIA
ANGELS

From the penthouse (the AL pennant) to the depths (sixth in the west) doesn't take long. The Angels proved it last year. To get back into the hunt (they finished 31 games out in '80), management was prepared to gamble.

The gamble doesn't look bad. The newest Angels know each other very well, thank you. They're the left side of the Boston Red Sox infield — SS Rick Burleson and 3B Butch Hobson. Hobson's exit from Beantown was no surprise; Burleson's was. The price: IF Carney Lansford (.261), OF Rick Miller (.274), and P Mark Clear (11-11). All should fit in well in Boston.

The addition of Burleson fills one important Angel need. California worked hard on the others: starting pitching, a strong-arm catcher, and a speedy centerfielder. Some of the holes were bound to be filled by opening day.

Clear's clear-out leaves the bullpen to Andy Hassler (5-1) and Don Aase (8-13) who excelled late in the season. The starters were, at best, so-so. A healthy Frank Tanana (11-12) will help.

Rod Carew, now 35, hasn't forgotten how to hit (.331, 34 doubles, both club records). Miller was the Angels' best outfielder last year. Neither Joe Rudi (.237) nor injured Don Baylor (.250) were able to do the job.

AL West
MINNESOTA TWINS

"We need a left-handed reliever and some right-handed power," said Twins' manager Johnny Goryl during the off-season. So did a lot of other big-league managers. But unless the team pulls some springtime surprises, Goryl is no better off than he was last year.

The lefty reliever would go nicely with bullpen righty Doug Corbett (8-6, 1.98 ERA, 23 saves). Lefty Jerry Koosman, now 37 years old, continues to please Minnesota fans with his 16-13 mark. Righty Roger Erickson fashioned a lowly 7-13 mark but with a 3.25 ERA. Rookie Al Williams opened with a fancy 6-2 mark. Manager Goryl's pitching is adequate.

Catcher Butch Wynegar (.255) does a solid job. And 3B John Castino (.302) and SS Roy Smalley (.278) give the Twins a solid left side. Trouble is, Castino's home run (13) and RBI (64) totals were the team's best. Hence the plea for more power.

Much improved OF Ken Landreaux gave the Twins a 100% effort on the way to his .281, 62 RBI season. Young Gary Ward, playing LF part-time in September, impressed with his .463 bat mark in 13 games.

On paper, the Twins are an average club that might duplicate its 77-84 mark in '80.

Chet Lemon

AL West
CHICAGO WHITE SOX

While their American League West rivals spent the winter finding new (and hopefully better) players, the Chisox tried to find a new owner (hopefully, one with a pile of money). The No. 1 candidate, Edward DeBartolo, Sr., struck out trying to win AL approval.

Meanwhile, the Sox weren't exactly sitting still. The major pickup, ex-Montreal (and Tiger) speed-demon Ron LeFlore (.257, but a National League high 97 steals). When Ron comes to play, he's dynamite.

The newest addition may do something to bolster Chicago's outstanding mound staff, otherwise known as "Those Young lefties." Six-five, 215-pound Britt Burns was the best of the lot in '80, compiling a 15-13 mark for a 70-90 club. Steve Trout (9-16) was impressive at times. Rich Wortham (4-7) should improve. Righty 6-5, 205-pounder Ed Farmer was the bullpen king with his 7-9, 30 saves 3.34 ERA performance.

Sox batters left something to be desired — and probably will again in '81. OF Chet Lemon (.292) is a solid pro. Rookie Harold Baines (.255) shows promise. Mike Squires (.283) and Lamar Johnson (.277) are set too.

59

AL West
SEATTLE MARINERS

Maury Wills never did anything the easy way. He clawed his way up through the Dodger farm system to become one of baseball's all-time great base thieves. Now, as manager of the lowly Mariners, he has a club that's short on both talent and money. A tough combination.

Maury starts with a decent, but not deep, pitching staff. The '80 team's ERA fell to 4.38, the fourth straight improvement in that department. Twelve wins by righty Glenn Abbott, the ace of the staff, matched his career high. Lefty Floyd Bannister went 9-13 for a 59-103 club. But his 3.47 ERA was the team's best and his 155 strikeouts made him fourth in the AL. A quartet of former Ranger pitchers, including ex-Yankee Ken Clay (2-3), may help.

The fifth Ranger to join Seattle in a 10-player deal becomes the Mariners' first real power man. He's Richie Zisk, who banged 19 homers while hitting .290 for Texas last year. He joins 1B Bruce Bochte (.300, 78 RBIs), the Seattle MVP, outfielders Dan Meyer (.275) and Tom Paciorek (.273), and speedy 2B Julio Cruz (.209, but 45 steals despite missing 44 games with injuries).

Look for Seattle to run, run, run. They stole 62 bases in the last 58 games — under manager Wills — last year.

NATIONAL LEAGUE
1980 STANDINGS

East

	Won	Lost	Pct.	GB
Philadelphia	91	71	.562	—
Montreal	90	72	.556	1
Pittsburgh	83	79	.512	8
St. Louis	74	88	.457	17
New York	67	95	.414	24
Chicago	64	98	.395	27

West

	Won	Lost	Pct.	GB
Houston	93	70	.571	—
Los Angeles	92	71	.564	1
Cincinnati	89	73	.549	3½
Atlanta	81	80	.503	11
San Francisco	75	86	.466	17
San Diego	73	89	.451	19½

TIE GAME: San Diego at Cincinnati, June 9, 11 innings (6-6)

and Previews for 1981

NL East
MONTREAL EXPOS

Does anyone remember the second-place finisher at the Miss America contest? Of course not. It's the same in baseball. The winners go to the playoffs and World Series. The losers — as the Expos have been in the final hours of the last two seasons — go home.

Manager Dick Williams is determined to avoid a repeat in '81, though the presence of the World Champion Phillies in the same NL East division will make it tough.

Tireless, All-Pro catcher Gary Carter (.264) is the NL's best, though he needs help. CF Andre Dawson (.308, the Expos' second-best ever) leads an outfield minus problem-child Ron LeFlore (.257, 97 steals) but including switch-hitting Rodney Scott (.224, but .295 righty) and Ellis Valentine (.315). Chris Speier (.265) showed a much-improved glove in '80. 3B Larry Parrish (.254) missed the month of June with a wrist injury. The Parrish and Valentine injuries (Ellis missed 77 games with a broken cheek) probably cost Montreal the '80 flag.

Young pitchers Scott Sanderson (16-11) and Bill Gullickson (10-5) are the keys to Montreal's questionable pitching, including ancient Woodie Fryman (7-4) and Steve Rogers (16-11).

NL East
PHILADELPHIA PHILLIES

It took nearly 100 years, but Cinderella finally got to wear the glass slipper in Philadelphia. Whether Dallas Green's Phils, who survived a summer of name-calling and unfriendliness, can keep the slipper in Veterans Stadium is another question.

Though aging 1B Pete Rose (.282 in all 162 games) is Philly's spiritual leader, the main man on the field is All-Pro 3B Mike Schmidt (.286, 48 homers, 121 RBIs). Pete and Mike cover the corners beautifully. Though Manny Trillo (.292) was the NL's best second-sacker a year ago, 35-year-old Larry Bowa (.267) showed signs of slippage. It may have been his last Philly season. The outfield, with young Lonnie Smith (.339 in 100 games) and Bake McBride (.309), can cover for lumbering Greg Luzinski (.228). Del Unser (.264) was the premier pinch-hitter in '80 and catcher Bob Boone (.229) was okay.

Lefty Carlton (24-9) continues as baseball's No. 1 flinger, but the rest of Philly's pitching may be suspect. Prime reliever Tug McGraw (5-4, 20 saves) is back in the bullpen along with rangy Ron Reed (7-5, nine saves). Bob Walk (11-7) and Dick Ruthven (17-10) can do the job.

Rookies to watch: P Mark Davis, SS Luis Aguayo, OF Bob Dernier.

NL East
ST. LOUIS CARDINALS

The most important person in the Card operation in '81 may be the guy selling programs. With Whitey Herzog serving as both field and general manager, the Cards made off-season deals like they were going out of style.

Did they help? Maybe. The newest Cards in Whitey's deck include ex-Cub super reliever Bruce Sutter (5-8, but a 2.65 ERA), former Padres P Bob Shirley (11-12, 3.55) and C-1B Gene Tenace (.222), and old Brewers OF Sixto Lezcano (.229, 18 homers), P Lary Sorenson (12-10), and a pair of top-rated Milwaukee farmhands.

No doubt the Cards will miss C Ted Simmons (.303), their most consistent hitter of the last decade, who left during the Brewer exchange. (Ex-Royal Darrell Porter replaces him.)

Other familiar names gone: OF Leon Durham (.271) and 3B Ken Reitz (.270) to Chicago; four pitchers, young catcher Terry Kennedy (.254), and two more players to San Diego; and P Rollie Fingers (11-9, 2.80, but shuffled through St. Louis) and P Pete Vuckovich (12-9) to Milwaukee. Chances are your favorite Cardinals are now working elsewhere.

That's not really fair, of course. All-Pro SS Garry Templeton (.319) and 1B Keith Hernandez (.321) lead the Card batters (who hit .275, best in the NL, last year).

Mike Easler

PITTSBURGH PIRATES

Pirate fans sat quietly last September as the team began to age in front of their eyes. Though the Bucs finished third, only eight games behind the champion Phils, they clearly weren't swaggering Pirates of the '70s.

They began dismantling the old machine when they sent P Bert Blyleven (8-13) to Cleveland along with aging C Manny Sanguillen (.250 in only 47 games). The new Bucs: starter Bob Owchinko (2-9) and reliever Victor Cruz (6-7) and catcher Gary Alexander (.225). None of the three are expected to turn the team around.

Not that there's no talent in Pittsburgh. Young LF Mike Easlier hit .338 and displayed good speed and fine power. RF Dave Parker slipped to .295 with 17 homers and 79 RBIs. But he's still a sight to behold at the plate. 1B (most of the time) John Milner can do better than .244. SS Tim Foli, the subject of numerous trade rumors, slid to .265 (from .291) but is still the heart of any team. 3B Bill Madlock, one of baseball's best hitters, sat out a long suspension for tangling with an umpire, then slumped to .277.

All-Pro Jim Bibby (19-6, 3.33) carried the Bucs until the very end. Eddie Solomon (7-3) turned in a nifty 2.70 ERA. Kent Tekulve, the bullpen ace, struggled to an 8-12, 21 saves finish.

Neil Allen

NEW YORK METS

The Mets, who escaped the east cellar only through the courtesy of the pitiful Cubs, promised all sorts of changes for 1981. But midway through the off-season, little had been done. Stay tuned — because the Mets' new owners mean business.

Barring last-second changes, manager Joe Torre faces a bleak future. The Mets uncovered a couple of fine youngsters last year, but they proved to be the team's only tradable material.

Reliever Neil Allen (7-10, 22 saves) was outstanding for a 67-95 team. Rookie Mark Bomback (10-8) was the only double-figure winner, but his 4.09 ERA was unimpressive. Craig Swan's continuing shoulder problem does not bode well for '81.

2B Doug Flynn (.255) held the Mets infield together. He won a Gold Glove. CF-1B Lee Mazzilli, who had problems on defense, hit .280 (with 16 homers, 76 RBIs, and 41 steals) after flirting with .300 late in the season. LF Steve Henderson led the league in hitting (.349) early, before sinking to .290. C Alex Trevino (.256) filled in nicely after an injury to John Stearns — who probably won't be with the club next season.

NL East
CHICAGO CUBS

The Cubbies figured that they couldn't win with premier reliever Bruce Sutter (28 saves and five wins among Chicago's 64 total victories). So now they'll try to win without him.

The off-season trade which brought Cardinals' Ken Reitz and Leon Durham to the Cubs solidifies two positions — third base and the outfield. And manager Joe Amalfitano was trying to lose some of his other high-priced, non-producing talent, like slugger Dave Kingman, as well. When you're 64-98, you might as well clean house.

Chicago pitching was horrible in '80. The team's 3.89 ERA proves it. Top winner Lynn McGlothen was 12-14 with a 4.80 earned run mark. Rick Reuschel (11-13) is better than his record shows. Dick Tidrow (6-5) leads the bullpen crew.

1B Billy Buckner, playing hurt, still led the NL in hitting (.324). He's solid. But the other Cubs didn't hit (a .251 team mark), a major factor in their last-place finish. C Tim Blackwell was adequate (.272). Ex-Red OF Hector Cruz replaces Mike Vail.

Chicago should still hold up the NL East.

Rookies to watch: OF Jim Tracy, OF Carlos Lezcano, P Randy Martz, P Lee Smith.

Nolan Ryan

NL WEST
HOUSTON ASTROS

Houston's biggest problem this off-season was figuring out who was running the team. That problem settled, the Astros can go about the business of defending their NL West championship. Their chances are excellent.

The addition of ex-Dodger Don Sutton (13-5) gives the Astros the best pitching staff in captivity. Despite the loss of J. R. Richard (10-4) and Nolan Ryan (11-10) late last season, Houston's mound staff carried the club to the west title. Righties Joe Niekro (20-12), Vern Ruhle (12-4), and Ken Forsch (12-13) paced the Astros to a league-leading 3.10 team ERA. Ex-Giant lefty Bob Knepper strengthens the rotation, and lefty reliever Joe Sambito (8-4, 17 saves) is super.

Though Joe Morgan (.243) was released and Enos Cabell (.276) was traded, the Astros are in great shape, with Art Howe (.283) and young Danny Heep (.276) battling at first and little Rafael Landestoy (.247) and Craig Reynolds (.226) anchoring the infield.

A healthy-again Cesar Cedeno (.309, but only 73 RBIs) and vet Jose Cruz (.302) are the outfield leaders, with Terry Puhl (.282) and Denny Walling (.299) just as solid.

Houston may be able to go all the way in '81.

NL WEST
LOS ANGELES DODGERS

Tom Lasorda's club finished second the hardest way of all last season — in a one-game playoff the day after the regular season ended. L. A.'s late rally — they won six of their last eight — came up just a hair short, a situation Lasorda intends to correct in '81.

It may be tough. Houston's pitching staff is stronger than ever, including the addition of ex-Dodger Don Sutton (13-5). But don't cry for L. A. Young Bob Welch (14-9), Jerry Reuss (18-6, after 7-14 in 1979), and Burt Hooton (14-8) are all solid. Top rookie Steve Howe (7-9, but 17 saves) was a super bullpen find.

The Dodgers can almost bank on 1B Steve Garvey's 200 hits and .300 average. He made both standards in '80, all routine for the All-pro vet. 2B Davey Lopes (.251), SS Bill Russell (.264), and 3B Ron Cey (.254) are all solid, though not the superstars they once promised to be.

The outfield is in super shape. The injured Reggie Smith (hitting .322 through 92 games a year ago) is back and healthy. And Dodger MVP Dusty Baker, armed with a new five-year contract, is ready to duplicate his .294, 97-ribbie season. Speedy Rudy Law (.260) and Pete Guerrero (.322) will anchor the Dodger outfield for years. Catching remains a question mark.

NL West
ATLANTA BRAVES

An 81-80 record usually isn't much to shout about. But in Atlanta, where the Braves turned in the one-better-than-even mark last season, there was mild rejoicing. It was the team's best record since 1974.

The Atlanta heroes came in a variety of shapes, sizes, and positions. Relief hurler Rick Camp (6-4) was brilliant with 22 saves and a 1.92 ERA. CF Dale Murphy (.281) had a super year (33 homers), and 3B Bob Horner bounced back from a snail-like start (owner Ted Turner wanted to ship him to Richmond) to hit .268 with 35 homers and 89 RBIs in only 124 games. 1B Chris Chambliss, the ex-Yankee, hit .282 and stroked a career-high 18 homers.

The problem with the Braves, however, is lack of bat power. The team average was only .250, 11th in the league. Shortstop Luis Gomez is a perfect example. The slick-fielder hit only .191 with only six extra-base blows.

Things are a little better in the Braves' pitching department. Ancient knuckleballer Phil Niekro (15-18) may go on forever, though he gave up 30 homers. Ex-Giant John Montefusco (obtained for Doyle Alexander) should fit in nicely. Tommy Boggs (12-9, 3.42) is just fine and No. 2 reliever Larry Bradford (3-4, 2.45) backs up Camp.

70

NL West
SAN FRANCISCO GIANTS

The most surprising move of the 1980 winter baseball meetings? It wasn't a trade. It wasn't a free-agent signing. It was a firing. The Giants sacked manager Dave Bristol — without so much as a hint in the nation's press.

The new man inherits a decent nucleus from the 75-86 1980 Giants. OF Jack Clark, whose .284 average should improve, led the NL in game-winning hits with 18. That means the 25-year-old accounted for nearly one of every four Giant wins. Lefty hurler Vida Blue deserved better than a 14-10 record off his 3.04 ERA. Still, 1980 marked Blue's eighth straight season with 14 or more wins. Ex-Brave Doyle Alexander should be a winner.

On the whole, Giant pitching is solid. The 3.46 team ERA was fourth in the NL and equal to AL Oakland's league-leading mark. Lefty Bob Knepper (9-16) is gone to Houston, but Houston's Enos Cabell, now a Giant, should really contribute for his new club.

San Francisco's infield is in excellent shape with Cabell joining Darrell Evans (.263), Mike Ivie (.241 in only 79 games), and Rennie Stennett (.245). Outside of Clark, the outfield is a trouble spot, though Terry Whitfield (.296) and Jim Wohlford (.280) can club the ball.

NL West
CINCINNATI REDS

Give credit to Reds' manager John McNamara. With slightly above-average hitting and slightly below-average pitching, he managed to keep his club in the division pennant race until the final days of the 1980 season. With few changes and with his players a year older, Mac will have to work some wonders to do as well in 1981.

OF Dave Collins (.303) was the team's only full-time .300 hitter. His outfield mates, Ken Griffey (.294) and George Foster (.273) knocked in 175 runs between them. The trio actually did more than their share. Ex-cub OF Mike Vail swings a big bat.

C Johnny Bench (.250) played in only 114 games a year ago. The one-time regular All-Pro wants to catch no more than 70-80 games a year from now on. That doesn't sit well with McNamara. 1B Dan Driessen (.265, 74 RBIs) played hurt and 3B Ray Knight (.264, 78 RBIs) has played better. SS Davey Concepcion (.260) is good but no longer great.

P Tom Seaver (10-8) doesn't overpower people anymore. But Mario Soto (10-8, 3.08) and Frank Pastore (13-7, 3.26) have proven themselves, and reliever Tom Hume (9-10, 2.56) was credited with 25 saves, second in the NL only to Bruce Sutter.

NL West
SAN DIEGO PADRES

Following a sad 1980 season, the Padres sent manager Jerry Coleman back to the broadcast booth he came from. His replacement: huge Frank Howard, the one-time Washington Senators strongboy.

Newcomer Howard is in good company. Many of the players are newcomers too. San Diego sent old favorites like relief ace Rollie Fingers (11-9, 23 saves), pitcher Bob Shirley (11-12), and first-sacker Gene Tenace (.222) to St. Louis for a quarter of a team — including pitchers John Urrea, John Littlefield, Al Olmsted, and Kim Seaman, catchers Terry Kennedy and Steve Swisher, and infielder Mike Phillips. With slugger Dave Winfield (.276, 87 RBIs) gone via the multi-million dollar free-agent route, manager Howard is really starting fresh.

Coleman didn't exactly leave a bare cupboard for his successor. The Padres were one of baseball's running-est clubs in '80, led by OF Gene Richards (.301, 193 hits, 61 steals, 20 outfield assists). OF Jerry Mumphrey (.298) had a brilliant second half, hitting .328 with 39 ribbies in the last 81 Padre games. SS Ozzie Smith (.230) sparkled in the field.

Can San Diego improve its 73-89 mark? Probably.

HOW THEY'LL FINISH IN 1981

National League East
1. Montreal Expos
2. Philadelphia Phillies
3. St. Louis Cardinals
4. Pittsburgh Pirates
5. New York Mets
6. Chicago Cubs

National League West
1. Houston Astros
2. Los Angeles Dodgers
3. Atlanta Braves
4. San Francisco Giants
5. Cincinnati Reds
6. San Diego Padres

American League East
1. New York Yankees
2. Milwaukee Brewers
3. Baltimore Orioles
4. Detroit Tigers
5. Boston Red Sox
6. Cleveland Indian's
7. Toronto Blue Jays

American League West
1. Kansas City Royals
2. Texas Rangers
3. Oakland A's
4. California Angels
5. Minnesota Twins
6. Chicago White Sox
7. Seattle Mariners

American League Champions: Kansas City Royals
National League Champions: Montreal Expos
World Champions: Kansas City Royals

1980 STATISTICS
AMERICAN LEAGUE
Batting
(140 or more at-bats)
*Bats Left-handed †Switch-Hitter

Batter and Club	AVG	G	AB	R	H	HR	RBI	SB
Adams, Glenn, Minn.*	.286	99	262	32	75	6	38	2
Aikens, Willie, K.C.*	.278	151	543	70	151	20	98	1
Alexander, Gary, Clev.	.225	76	178	22	40	5	31	0
Anderson, Jim, Sea.	.227	116	317	46	72	8	30	2
Armas, Tony, Oak	.279	158	628	87	175	35	109	5
Aujt, Doug, Tor.	.194	64	144	12	28	3	15	0
Ayala, Benny, Balt.	.265	76	170	28	45	10	33	0
Bailor, Bob, Tor.	.236	117	347	44	82	1	16	12
Baines, Harold, Chgo.*	.255	141	491	55	125	13	49	2
Bando, Sal, Milw.	.197	78	254	28	50	5	31	5
Bannister, Alan, Chgo.-Clev.	.283	126	392	57	111	1	41	14
Baylor, Don, Calif.	.250	90	340	39	85	5	51	6
Belanger, Mark, Balt.	.228	113	268	37	61	0	22	6
Bell, Buddy, Tex.	.329	129	490	76	161	17	83	3
Bell, Kevin, Chgo.	.178	92	191	16	34	1	11	0
Beniquez, Juan, Sea.	.228	70	237	26	54	6	21	2
Bochte, Bruce, Sea.*	.300	148	520	62	156	13	78	2
Bonnell, Barry, Tor.	.268	130	463	55	124	13	56	3
Bosetti, Rick, Tor.	.213	53	188	24	40	4	18	4
Bosley, Thad, Chgo.*	.224	70	147	12	33	2	14	3
Brett, George, K.C.*	.390	117	449	87	175	24	118	15
Brohamer, Jack, Bos.-Clev.*	.251	74	199	18	50	2	21	0
Brookens, Tom, Det.	.275	151	509	64	140	10	66	13
Brown, Bobby, N.Y.†	.260	137	412	65	107	14	47	27
Bumbry, Al, Balt.*	.318	160	645	118	205	9	53	44
Burleson, Rick, Bos	.278	155	644	89	179	8	51	12
Campaneris, Bert, Calif	.252	77	210	32	53	2	18	10
Carew, Rod, Calif.*	.331	144	540	74	179	3	59	23

75

Batter and Club	AVG	G	AB	R	H	HR	RBI	SB
Castino, John, Minn.	.302	150	546	67	165	13	64	7
Cerone, Rick, N.Y.	.277	147	519	70	144	14	85	1
Chalk, Dave, K.C.	.251	69	167	19	42	1	20	1
Charboneau, Joe, Clev.	.289	131	453	76	131	23	87	2
Clark, Bob, Calif.	.230	78	261	26	60	5	23	0
Cooper, Cecil, Milw.*	.352	153	622	96	219	25	122	17
Corcoran, Tim, Det.*	.288	84	153	20	44	3	18	0
Cowens, Al, Calif.-Det.	.268	142	522	69	140	6	59	6
Cox, Jeff, Oak.	.213	59	169	20	36	0	9	8
Cox, Larry, Sea.	.202	105	243	18	49	4	20	1
Cox, Ted, Sea.	.243	83	247	17	60	2	23	0
Craig, Rodney, Sea.†	.238	70	240	30	57	3	20	3
Crowley, Terry, Balt.*	.288	92	233	33	67	12	50	0
Cruz, Julio, Sea.†	.209	119	422	66	88	2	16	45
Cruz, Todd, Calif.-Chgo.	.237	108	333	28	79	3	23	2
Cubbage, Mike, Minn.*	.246	103	285	29	70	8	42	0
Dauer, Rich, Balt.	.284	152	557	71	158	2	63	3
Davis, Bob, Tor.	.216	91	218	18	47	4	19	0
Davis, Dick, Milw.	.271	106	365	50	99	4	30	5
DeCinces, Doug, Balt.	.249	145	489	64	122	16	64	11
Dempsey, Rick, Balt.	.262	119	362	51	95	9	40	3
Dent, Bucky, N.Y.	.262	141	489	57	128	5	52	0
Diaz, Bo, Clev.	.227	76	207	15	47	3	32	1
Dilone, Miguel, Clev.†	.341	132	528	82	180	0	40	61
Donohue, Tom, Calif.	.188	84	218	18	41	2	14	5
Dwyer, Jim, Bos.*	.285	93	260	41	74	9	38	3
Dybzinski, Jerry, Clev.	.230	114	248	32	57	1	23	4
Edwards, Dave, Minn.	.250	81	200	26	50	2	20	2
Ellis, John, Tex.	.236	73	182	12	43	1	23	3
Essian, Jim, Oak.	.232	87	285	19	66	5	29	1
Evans, Dwight, Bos.	.266	148	463	72	123	18	60	3
Fisk, Carlton, Bos.	.289	131	478	73	138	18	62	11
Ford, Dan, Calif.	.279	65	226	22	63	7	26	0
Frias, Pepe, Tex.	.242	116	227	27	55	0	10	5
Gamble, Oscar, N.Y.*	.278	78	194	40	54	14	50	2
Gantner, Jim, Milw.*	.282	132	415	47	117	4	40	11
Garcia, Damaso, Tor.	.278	140	543	50	151	4	46	13
Garcia, Kiko, Balt.	.199	111	311	27	62	1	27	8
Gibson, Kirk, Det.*	.263	51	175	23	46	9	16	4
Graham, Dan, Balt.*	.278	86	266	32	74	15	54	0

Batter and Club	AVG	G	AB	R	H	HR	RBI	SB
Grich, Bobby, Calif.	.271	150	498	60	135	14	62	3
Griffin, Alfredo, Tor.†	.254	155	653	63	166	2	41	18
Gross, Wayne, Oak.*	.281	113	366	45	103	14	61	5
Grubb, John, Tex.*	.277	110	274	40	76	9	32	2
Guerrero, Mario, Oak.	.239	116	381	32	91	2	23	3
Hargrove, Mike, Clev.*	.304	160	589	86	179	11	85	4
Harlow, Larry, Calif.*	.276	109	301	47	83	4	27	3
Harrah, Toby, Clev.	.267	160	561	100	150	11	72	17
Harrelson, Bud, Tex.†	.272	87	180	26	49	1	9	4
Hassey, Ron, Clev.*	.318	130	390	43	124	8	65	0
Heath, Mike, Oak.	.243	92	305	27	74	1	33	3
Hebner, Richie, Det.*	.290	104	341	48	99	12	82	0
Henderson, Rickey, Oak.	.303	158	591	111	179	9	53	100
Hobson, Butch, Bos.	.228	93	324	35	74	11	39	1
Hoffman, Glenn, Bos.	.285	114	312	37	89	4	42	2
Horton, Willie, Sea.	.221	97	335	32	74	8	36	0
Howell, Roy, Tor.*	.269	142	528	51	142	10	57	0
Hurdle, Clint, K.C.*	.294	130	395	50	116	10	60	0
Iorg, Garth, Tor.	.248	80	222	24	55	2	14	2
Jackson, Reggie, N.Y.*	.300	143	514	94	154	41	111	1
Jackson, Ron, Minn.	.265	131	396	48	105	5	42	1
Johnson, Cliff, Clev.	.230	54	174	25	40	6	28	0
Johnson, Lamar, Chgo.	.277	147	541	51	150	13	81	1
Jones, Ruppert, N.Y.*	.223	83	328	38	73	9	42	18
Kelly, Harold Pat, Balt.*	.260	89	200	38	52	3	26	16
Kemp, Steve, Det.*	.293	135	508	88	149	21	101	5
Kimm, Bruce, Chgo.	.243	100	251	20	61	0	19	1
Klutts, Mickey, Oak.	.269	75	197	20	53	4	21	1
Kuiper, Duane, Clev.*	.282	42	149	10	42	0	9	0
LaCock, Pete, K.C.*	.205	114	156	14	32	1	18	1
Landreaux, Ken, Minn.*	.281	129	484	56	136	7	62	8
Lansford, Carney, Calif.	.261	151	602	87	157	15	80	14
Lefebvre, Joe, N.Y.*	.227	74	150	26	34	8	21	0
Lemon, Chet, Chgo.	.292	146	514	76	150	11	51	6
Lentine, Jim, Det.	.261	67	161	19	42	1	17	2
Lezcano, Sixto, Milw.	.229	112	411	51	94	18	55	1
Lowenstein, John, Balt.*	.311	104	196	38	61	4	27	7
Lynn, Fred, Bos.*	.301	110	415	67	125	12	61	12
Mackanin, Pete, Minn.	.266	108	319	31	85	4	35	6
Manning, Rick, Clev.*	.234	140	471	55	110	3	52	12

Batter and Club	AVG	G	AB	R	H	HR	RBI	SB
Martinez, Buck, Milw.	.224	76	219	16	49	3	17	1
May, Lee, Balt.	.243	78	222	20	54	7	31	2
Mayberry, John, Tor.*	.248	149	501	62	124	30	82	0
McKay, Dave, Oak.†	.244	123	295	29	72	1	29	1
McRae, Hal, K.C.	.297	124	489	73	145	14	83	10
Mendoza, Mario, Sea.	.245	114	277	27	68	2	14	3
Meyer, Dan, Sea.*	.275	146	531	56	146	11	71	8
Milbourne, Larry, Sea.†	.264	106	258	31	68	0	26	7
Miller, Rick, Calif.*	.274	129	412	52	113	2	38	7
Molinaro, Bob, Chgo.*	.291	119	344	48	100	5	36	18
Molitor, Paul, Milw.	.304	111	450	81	137	9	37	34
Money, Don, Milw.	.256	86	289	39	74	17	46	0
Moore, Charlie, Milw.	.291	111	320	42	93	2	30	10
Morales, Jose, Minn.	.303	97	241	36	73	8	36	0
Morrison, Jim, Chgo.	.283	162	604	66	171	15	57	8
Moseby, Lloyd, Tor.*	.229	114	389	44	89	9	46	4
Murcer, Bobby, N.Y.*	.269	100	297	41	80	13	57	2
Murphy, Dwayne, Oak.*	.274	159	573	86	157	13	68	26
Murray, Eddie, Balt.†	.300	158	621	100	186	32	116	7
Nettles, Graig, N.Y.*	.244	89	324	52	79	16	45	0
Newman, Jeff, Oak.	.233	127	438	37	102	15	56	3
Nordhagen, Wayne, Chgo.	.277	123	415	45	115	15	59	0
Norris, Jim, Tex.*	.247	119	174	23	43	0	16	6
Oglivie, Ben, Milw.*	.304	156	592	94	180	41	118	11
Oliver, Al, Tex.*	.319	163	656	96	209	19	117	5
Orta, Jorge, Clev.*	.291	129	481	78	140	10	64	6
Otis, Amos, K.C.	.251	107	394	56	99	10	53	16
Paciorek, Tom, Sea.	.273	126	418	44	114	15	59	3
Page, Mitchell, Oak.*	.244	110	348	58	85	17	51	14
Parrish, Lance, Det.	.286	144	553	79	158	24	82	6
Patek, Fred, Calif.	.264	86	273	41	72	5	34	7
Perez, Tony, Box.	.275	151	585	73	161	25	105	1
Peters, Rick, Det.†	.291	133	477	79	139	2	42	13
Picciolo, Rob, Oak.	.240	95	271	32	65	5	18	1
Piniella, Lou, N.Y.	.287	116	321	39	92	2	27	0
Porter, Darrell, K.C.*	.249	118	418	51	104	7	51	1
Powell, Hosken, Minn.*	.262	137	485	58	127	6	35	14
Pryor, Greg, Chgo.	.240	122	338	32	81	1	29	2
Putnam, Pat, Tex.*	.263	147	410	42	108	13	55	0
Quirk, Jamie, K.C.*	.276	62	163	13	45	5	21	3

Batter and Club	AVG	G	AB	R	H	HR	RBI	SB
Randolph, Willie, N.Y.	.294	138	513	99	151	7	46	30
Remy, Jerry, Bos.*	.313	63	230	24	72	0	9	14
Revering, Dave, Oak.*	.290	106	376	48	109	15	62	1
Rice, Jim, Bos.	.294	124	504	81	148	24	86	8
Rivers, Mickey, Tex.*	.333	147	630	96	210	7	60	18
Roberts, Dave, Tex.	.238	101	235	27	56	10	30	0
Roberts, Leon, Sea.	.251	119	374	48	94	10	33	8
Rodriguez, Aurelio, N.Y.	.220	52	164	14	36	3	14	0
Roenicke, Gary, Balt.	.239	118	297	40	71	10	28	2
Rudi, Joe, Calif.	.237	104	372	42	88	16	53	1
Sample, Billy, Tex.	.260	99	204	29	53	4	19	8
Simpson, Joe, Sea.*	.249	129	365	42	91	3	34	17
Singleton, Ken, Balt.†	.304	156	583	85	177	24	104	0
Smalley, Roy, Minn.†	.278	133	486	64	35	12	63	3
Soderholm, Eric, N.Y.	.287	95	275	38	79	11	35	0
Sofield, Rick, Minn.*	.247	131	417	52	103	9	49	4
Spencer, Jim, N.Y.*	.236	97	259	38	61	13	43	1
Squires, Mike, Chgo.*	.283	131	343	38	97	2	33	8
Stapleton, Dave, Bos.	.321	106	449	61	144	7	45	3
Staub, Rusty, Tex.*	.300	109	340	42	102	9	55	1
Stein, Bill, Sea.	.268	67	198	16	53	5	27	1
Summers, Champ, Det.*	.297	120	347	61	103	17	60	4
Sundberg, Jim, Tex.	.273	151	505	59	138	10	63	2
Thomas, Gorman, Milw.	.239	162	628	78	150	38	105	8
Thompson, Jason, Det.-Calif.*	.288	138	438	69	126	21	90	2
Thon, Dickie, Calif.	.255	80	267	32	68	0	15	7
Trammell, Alan, Det.	.300	146	560	107	168	9	65	12
Velez, Otto, Tor.	.269	104	357	54	96	20	62	0
Veryzer, Tom, Clev.	.271	109	358	28	97	2	28	0
Washington, U.L., K.C.†	.273	153	549	79	150	6	53	20
Wathan, John, K.C.	.305	126	453	57	138	6	58	17
Watson, Bob, N.Y.	.307	130	469	62	144	13	68	2
Whitaker, Lou, Det.*	.233	145	477	68	111	1	45	8
White, Frank, K.C.	.264	154	560	70	148	7	60	19
Whitt, Ernie, Tor.*	.237	106	295	23	70	6	34	1
Wilfong, Rob, Minn.*	.248	131	416	55	103	8	45	10
Wills, Bump, Tex.†	.263	146	578	102	152	5	58	34
Wilson, Willie, K.C.†	.326	161	705	133	230	3	49	79
Wockenfuss, John, Det.	.274	126	372	56	102	16	65	1

Batter and Club	AVG	G	AB	R	H	HR	RBI	SB
Woods, Al, Tor.*	.300	109	373	54	112	15	47	4
Wynegar, Butch, Minn.†	.255	146	486	61	124	5	57	3
Yastrzemski, Carl, Bos.*	.275	105	364	49	100	15	50	0
Yount, Robin, Milw.	.293	143	611	121	179	23	87	20
Zisk, Richie, Tex.	.290	135	448	48	130	19	77	0

AMERICAN LEAGUE

Pitching

(75 or more innings)
*Pitches Left-handed

*Throws Lefthanded

Pitcher and Club	W	L	ERA	G	IP	H	BB	SO
Aase, Don, Calif.	8	13	4.06	40	175	193	66	74
Abbott, Glenn, Sea.	12	12	4.10	31	215	228	49	78
Arroyo, Fernando, Minn.	6	6	4.70	21	92	97	32	27
Bannister, Floyd, Sea.*	9	13	3.47	32	218	200	66	155
Barker, Len, Clev.	19	12	4.17	36	246	237	92	187
Baumgarten, Ross, Chgo.*	2	12	3.44	24	136	127	52	66
Beattie, Jim, Sea.	5	15	4.86	33	187	205	98	67
Burns, Britt, Chgo.*	15	13	2.84	34	238	213	63	133
Caldwell, Mike, Milw.*	13	11	4.04	34	225	248	56	74
Clancy, Jim, Tor.	13	16	3.30	34	251	217	128	152
Clear, Mark, Calif.	11	11	3.31	58	106	82	65	105
Cleveland, Reggie, Milw.	11	9	3.74	45	154	150	49	54
Corbett, Doug, Minn.	8	6	1.99	73	136	102	42	89
Cruz, Victor, Clev.	6	7	3.45	55	86	71	27	88
Darwin, Danny, Tex.	13	4	2.62	53	110	98	50	104
Davis, Ron, N.Y.	9	3	2.95	53	131	121	32	65
Denny, John, Clev.	8	6	4.38	16	109	116	47	59
Dotson, Richard, Chgo.	12	10	4.27	33	198	185	87	109
Drago, Dick, Bos.	7	7	4.13	43	133	127	44	63
Dressler, Rob, Sea.	4	10	3.99	30	149	161	33	50
Eckersley, Dennis, Bos.	12	14	4.27	30	198	188	44	121
Erickson, Roger, Minn.	7	13	3.25	32	191	198	56	97
Farmer, Ed, Chgo.	7	9	3.33	64	100	92	56	54
Figueroa, Ed, N.Y.-Tex.	3	10	6.52	23	98	152	36	25
Flanagan, Mike, Balt.*	16	13	4.12	37	251	278	71	128

Pitcher and Club	W	L	ERA	G	IP	H	BB	SO
Frost, Dave, Calif.	4	8	5.31	15	78	97	21	28
Gale, Rich, K.C.	13	9	3.91	32	191	169	78	97
Garland, Wayne, Clev.	6	9	4.62	25	150	163	48	55
Garvin, Jerry, Tor.*	4	7	2.28	61	83	70	27	52
Gossage, Rich, N.Y.	6	2	2.27	64	99	74	37	103
Grimsley, Ross, Clev.*	4	5	6.72	14	75	103	24	18
Guidry, Ron, N.Y.*	17	10	3.56	37	220	215	80	166
Gura, Larry, K.C.*	18	10	2.96	36	283	272	76	113
Haas, Moose, Milw.	16	15	3.11	33	252	246	56	146
Hassler, Andy, Calif.*	5	1	2.49	41	83	67	37	75
Heaverlo, Dave, Sea.	6	3	3.87	60	79	75	35	42
Honeycutt, Rick, Sea.*	10	17	3.95	30	203	221	60	79
Hoyt, Lamarr, Chgo.	9	3	4.58	24	112	123	41	55
Jackson, Darrell, Minn.*	9	9	3.87	32	172	161	69	90
Jefferson, Jesse, Tor.	4	13	5.46	29	122	130	52	53
Jenkins, Ferguson, Tex.	12	12	3.77	29	198	190	52	129
John, Tommy, N.Y.*	22	9	3.43	36	265	270	56	78
Keough, Matt, Oak.	16	13	2.92	34	250	218	94	121
Kingman, Brian, Oak.	8	20	3.84	32	211	209	82	116
Kison, Bruce, Calif.	3	6	4.93	13	73	73	32	28
Knapp, Chris, Calif.	2	11	6.15	32	117	133	51	46
Koosman, Jerry, Minn.*	16	13	4.04	38	243	252	69	149
Kravec, Ken, Chgo.*	3	6	6.91	20	82	100	44	37
LaRoche, Dave, Calif.*	3	5	4.08	52	128	122	39	89
Lacey, Bob, Oak.*	3	2	2.93	47	80	68	21	45
Langford, Rick, Oak.	19	12	3.26	35	290	276	64	102
Lemanczyk, Dave, Tor.-Calif.	4	9	4.79	31	109	138	42	29
Leonard, Dennis, K.C.	20	11	3.79	38	280	271	80	155
Lopez, Aurelio, Det.	13	6	3.77	67	124	125	45	97
Martin, Renie, K.C.	10	10	4.40	32	137	133	70	68
Martinez, Alfredo, Calif.	7	9	4.53	30	149	150	59	57
Martinez, Dennis, Balt.	6	4	3.96	25	100	103	44	42
Martinez, Tippy, Balt.*	4	4	3.00	52	81	69	34	68
Matlack, Jon, Tex.*	10	10	3.68	35	235	265	48	142
May, Rudy, N.Y.*	15	5	2.47	41	175	144	39	133
McCatty, Steve, Oak	14	14	3.85	33	222	202	99	114
McClure, Bob, Milw.*	5	8	3.07	52	91	83	37	47

Pitcher and Club	W	L	ERA	G	IP	H	BB	SO
McGregor, Scott, Balt.*	20	8	3.32	36	252	254	58	119
McLaughlin, Byron, Sea.	3	6	6.82	45	91	124	50	41
McLaughlin, Joey, Tor.	6	9	4.50	55	136	159	53	70
Medich, Doc, Tex.	14	11	3.93	34	204	230	56	91
Mirabella, Paul, Tor.*	5	12	4.33	33	131	151	66	53
Mitchell, Paul, Milw.	5	5	3.54	17	89	92	15	29
Monge, Sid, Clev.*	3	5	3.64	67	94	80	40	60
Montague, John, Calif.	4	2	5.11	37	74	97	21	22
Morris, Jack, Det.	16	15	4.18	36	250	252	87	112
Norris, Mike, Oak	22	9	2.54	33	284	215	83	180
Owchinko, Bob, Clev.*	2	9	5.29	29	114	138	47	66
Palmer, Jim, Balt.	16	10	3.98	34	224	238	74	109
Parrott, Mike, Sea.	1	16	7.28	27	94	136	42	53
Pattin, Marty, K.C.	4	0	3.64	37	89	97	23	40
Perry, Gaylord, Tex.-N.Y.	10	13	3.67	34	206	224	64	135
Petry, Dan, Det.	10	9	3.93	27	165	156	83	88
Proly, Mike, Chgo	5	10	3.06	62	147	136	58	56
Quisenberry, Dan, K.C.	12	7	3.09	75	128	129	27	37
Rainey, Chuck, Bos.	8	3	4.86	16	87	92	41	43
Rawley, Shane, Sea.*	7	7	3.32	59	114	103	63	68
Redfern, Pete, Minn.	7	7	4.54	23	105	117	33	73
Renko, Steve, Bos.	9	9	4.20	32	165	180	56	90
Roberts, Dave, Sea.*	2	3	4.39	37	80	86	27	47
Rozema, Dave, Det.	6	9	3.91	42	145	152	49	49
Schatzeder, Dan, Det.*	11	13	4.01	32	193	178	58	94
Sorensen, Lary, Milw.	12	10	3.67	35	196	242	45	54
Spillner, Dan, Clev.	16	11	5.29	34	194	225	74	100
Splittorff, Paul, K.C.*	14	11	4.15	34	204	236	43	53
Stanley, Bob, Bos.	10	8	3.39	52	175	186	52	71
Stanton, Mike, Clev.	1	3	5.34	51	86	98	44	74
Stewart, Sammy, Balt.	7	7	3.55	33	119	103	60	78
Stieb, Dave, Tor.	12	15	3.70	34	243	232	83	108
Stoddard, Tim, Balt.	5	3	2.51	64	86	72	38	64
Stone, Steve, Balt.	25	7	3.23	37	251	224	101	149
Tanana, Frank, Calif.*	11	12	4.15	32	204	223	45	113
Tiant, Luis, N.Y.	8	9	4.90	25	136	139	50	84
Todd, Jackson, Tor.	5	2	4.02	12	85	90	30	44
Torrez, Mike, Bos.	9	16	5.09	36	207	256	75	97

Pitcher and Club	W	L	ERA	G	IP	H	BB	SO
Travers, Billy, Milw.*	12	6	3.92	29	154	147	47	62
Trout, Steve, Chgo.*	9	16	3.69	32	200	229	49	89
Tudor, John, Bos.*	8	5	3.03	16	92	81	31	45
Underwood, Pat, Det.*	3	6	3.58	49	113	121	35	60
Underwood, Tom, N.Y.*	13	9	3.66	38	187	163	66	116
Verhoeven, John, Minn.	3	4	3.96	44	100	109	29	42
Waits, Rick, Clev.*	13	14	4.46	33	224	231	82	109
Wilcox, Milt, Det.	13	11	4.48	32	199	201	68	97
Williams, Albert, Minn.	6	2	3.51	18	77	73	30	35
Wortham, Richard, Chgo.*	4	7	5.97	41	92	102	58	45
Zahn, Geoff, Minn.*	14	18	4.40	38	233	273	66	96

NATIONAL LEAGUE

Batting

(65 or more at-bats)
*Bats Left-handed   †Switch-Hitter

Batter and Club	AVG	G	AB	R	H	HR	RBI	SB
Alexander, Doyle, Atl.	.181	35	83	7	15	0	3	0
Almon, William, Mtl.-N.Y.#	.193	66	150	15	29	0	7	2
Ashby, Alan, Hou.#	.256	116	352	30	90	3	48	0
Asselstine, Brian, Atl.*	.284	87	218	18	62	3	25	1
Aviles, Ramon, Phil.	.277	51	101	12	28	2	9	0
Backman, Walter, N.Y.#	.323	27	93	12	30	0	9	2
Baker, Johnnie, L.A.	.294	153	579	80	170	29	97	12
Bench, Johnny, Cin.	.250	114	360	52	90	24	68	4
Benedict, Bruce, Atl.	.253	120	359	18	91	2	34	3
Bergman, David, Hou.*	.256	90	78	12	20	0	3	1
Bernazard, Antonio, Mtl.#	.224	82	183	26	41	5	18	9
Berra, Dale, Pitt.	.220	93	245	21	54	6	31	2
Bevacqua, Kurt, S.D.-Pitt.	.228	84	114	5	26	0	16	1
Bibby, James, Pitt.	.156	35	77	6	12	1	7	0
Biittner, Larry, Chi.*	.249	127	273	21	68	1	34	1
Blackwell, Timothy, Chi.#	.272	103	320	24	87	5	30	0

Batter and Club	AVG	G	AB	R	H	HR	RBI	SB
Blanks, Larvell, Atl.	.204	88	221	23	45	2	12	1
Blue, Vida, S.F.*	.074	31	68	3	5	0	1	0
Bonds, Bobby, St.L.	.203	86	231	37	47	5	24	15
Boone, Robert, Phil.	.229	141	480	34	110	9	55	3
Bowa, Lawrence, Phil.#	.267	147	540	57	144	2	39	21
Breining, Fred, S.F.	—	5	0	0	0	0	0	0
Brooks, Hubert, N.Y.	.309	24	81	8	25	1	10	1
Buckner, William, Chi.*	.324	145	578	69	187	10	68	1
Burroughs, Jeffrey, Atl.	.263	99	278	35	73	13	51	1
Cabell, Enos, Hou.	.276	152	604	69	167	2	55	21
Candelaria, John, Pitt.*	.195	35	77	5	15	0	7	0
Carlton, Steven, Phil.*	.188	38	101	7	19	0	6	0
Carter, Gary, Mtl.	.264	154	549	76	145	29	101	3
Cash, David, S.D.	.227	130	397	25	90	1	23	6
Cedeno, Cesar, Hou.	.309	137	499	71	154	10	73	48
Cey, Ronald, L.A.	.254	157	551	81	140	28	77	2
Chambliss, C.								
Christopher, Atl.*	.282	158	602	83	170	18	72	7
Clark, Jack, S.F.	.284	127	437	77	124	22	82	2
Collins, David, Cin.#	.303	144	551	94	167	3	35	79
Concepcion, David, Cin.	.260	156	622	72	162	5	77	12
Cromartie, Warren, Mtl.*	.288	162	597	74	172	14	70	8
Cruz, Hector, Cin.	.213	52	75	5	16	1	5	0
Cruz, Jose, Hou.*	.302	160	612	79	185	11	91	36
Dawson, Andre, Mtl.	.308	151	577	96	178	17	87	34
DeJesus, Ivan, Chi.	.259	157	618	78	160	3	33	44
Dillard, Stephen, Chi.	.225	100	244	31	55	4	27	2
Driessen, Daniel, Cin.*	.265	154	524	81	139	14	74	19
Durham, Leon, St.L.*	.271	96	303	42	82	8	42	8
Easler, Michael, Pitt.*	.338	132	393	66	133	21	74	5
Evans, Barry, S.D.	.232	73	125	11	29	1	14	1
Evans, Darrell, S.F.*	.264	154	556	69	147	20	78	17
Fahey, William, S.D.*	.257	93	241	18	62	1	22	2
Ferguson, Joseph, L.A.	.238	77	172	20	41	9	29	2
Figueroa, Jesus, Chi.*	.253	115	198	20	50	1	11	2
Flannery, Timothy, S.D.*	.240	95	292	15	70	0	25	2
Flynn, R. Douglas, N.Y.	.255	128	443	46	113	0	24	2
Foli, Timothy, Pitt.	.265	127	495	61	131	3	38	11
Foote, Barry, Chi.	.238	63	202	16	48	6	28	1
Forsch, Kenneth, Hou.	.234	32	77	3	18	0	8	1

Batter and Club	AVG	G	AB	R	H	HR	RBI	SB
Forsch, Robert, St.L.	.295	32	78	11	23	3	10	1
Foster, George, Cin.	.273	144	528	79	144	25	93	1
Garner, Philip, Pitt.	.259	151	548	62	142	5	58	32
Garvey, Steven, L.A.	.304	163	658	78	200	26	106	6
Geronimo, Cesar, Cin.*	.255	103	145	16	37	2	9	2
Gomez, Luis, Atl.	.191	121	278	18	53	0	24	0
Griffey, G. Kenneth, Cin.*	.294	146	544	89	160	13	85	23
Gross, Gregory, Phil.*	.240	127	154	19	37	0	12	1
Guerrero, Pedro, L.A.	.322	75	183	27	59	7	31	2
Hatcher, Michael, L.A.	.226	57	84	4	19	1	5	0
Heep, Daniel, Hou.*	.276	33	87	6	24	0	6	0
Henderson, Kenneth, Chi.#	.195	44	82	7	16	2	9	0
Henderson, Stephen, N.Y.	.290	143	513	75	149	8	58	23
Hendrick, George, St.L.	.302	150	572	73	173	25	109	6
Hernandez, Keith, St.L.*	.321	159	595	111	191	16	99	14
Herndon, Larry, S.F.	.258	139	493	54	127	8	49	8
Herr, Thomas, St.L.#	.248	76	222	29	55	0	15	9
Horner, J. Robert, Atl.	.268	124	463	81	124	35	89	3
Howe, Arthur, Hou.	.283	110	321	34	91	10	46	1
Hubbard, Glenn, Atl.	.248	117	431	55	107	9	43	7
Iorg, Dane, St.L.*	.303	105	251	33	76	3	36	1
Ivie, Michael, S.F.	.241	79	286	21	69	4	25	1
Johnson, Clifford, Chi.	.235	68	196	28	46	10	34	0
Johnstone, John, L.A.*	.307	109	251	31	77	2	20	3
Jorgensen, Michael, N.Y.*	.255	119	321	43	82	7	43	0
Kelleher, Michael, Chi.	.146	105	96	12	14	0	4	1
Kennedy, Junior, Cin.	.261	104	337	31	88	1	34	3
Kennedy, Terrence, St.L.*	.254	84	248	28	63	4	34	0
Kingman, David, Chi.	.278	81	255	31	71	18	57	2
Knepper, Robert, S.F.*	.152	35	66	3	10	0	7	1
Knight, C. Ray, Cin.	.264	162	618	71	163	14	78	1
Krukow, Michael, Chi.	.246	34	65	5	16	1	6	0
Lacy, Leondaus, Pitt.	.335	109	278	45	93	7	33	18
Landestoy, Rafael, Hou.#	.247	149	393	42	97	1	27	23
Landrum, Terry, St.L.	.247	35	77	6	19	0	7	3
Law, Rudy, L.A.*	.260	128	388	55	101	1	23	40
Law, Vance, Pitt.	.230	25	74	11	17	0	3	2
LeFlore, Ronald, Mtl.	.257	139	521	95	134	4	39	97
LeMaster, Johnnie, S.F.	.215	135	405	33	87	3	31	0

Batter and Club	AVG	G	AB	R	H	HR	RBI	SB
Leonard, Jeffrey, Hou.......	.213	88	216	29	46	3	20	4
Lezcano, Carlos, Chi........	.205	42	88	15	18	3	12	1
Lopes, David, L.A...........	.251	141	553	79	139	10	49	23
Lum, Michael, Atl.*........	.205	93	83	7	17	0	5	0
Luzinski, Gregory, Phil.	.228	106	368	44	84	19	56	3
Macha, Kenneth, Mtl.	.290	49	107	10	31	1	8	0
Maddox, Elliott, N.Y.	.246	130	411	35	101	4	34	1
Maddox, Garry, Phil........	.259	143	549	59	142	11	73	25
Madlock, Bill, Pitt.	.277	137	494	62	137	10	53	16
Martin, Jerry, Chi.	.227	141	494	57	112	23	73	8
Matthews, Gary, Atl........	.278	155	571	79	159	19	75	11
May, Milton, S.F.*..........	.260	111	358	27	93	6	50	0
Mazzilli, Lee, N.Y.#	.280	152	578	82	162	16	76	41
McBride, Arnold, Phil.*	.309	137	554	68	171	9	87	13
McCovey, Willie, S.F.*	.204	48	113	8	23	1	16	0
Mejias, Samuel, Cin.	.278	71	108	16	30	1	10	4
Milner, John, Pitt.*	.244	114	238	31	58	8	34	2
Monday, Robert, L.A.*	.268	96	194	35	52	10	25	2
Montanez, Guillermo, S.D.-Mtl.*	.272	142	500	40	136	6	64	3
Montefusco, John, S.F.	.033	22	30	1	1	0	0	0
Morales, Julio, N.Y.	.254	94	193	19	49	3	30	2
Moreland, B. Keith, Phil.	.314	62	159	13	50	4	29	3
Moreno, Omar, Pitt.*.......	.249	162	676	87	168	2	36	96
Morgan, Joe, Hou.*	.243	141	461	66	112	11	49	24
Mumphrey, Jerry, S.D.#...	.298	160	564	61	168	4	59	52
Murphy, Dale, Atl............	.281	156	569	98	160	33	89	9
Murray, Richard, S.F.......	.216	53	194	19	42	4	24	2
Nahorodny, William, Atl. ...	.242	59	157	14	38	5	18	0
Nicosia, Steven, Pitt.	.216	60	176	16	38	1	22	0
Niekro, Joseph, Hou........	.275	37	80	7	22	0	10	0
Niekro, Philip, Atl.	.133	40	90	2	12	0	5	0
Nolan, Joseph, Atl.-Cin.* .	.307	70	176	16	54	3	26	0
Norman, Daniel, N.Y.#	.185	69	92	5	17	2	9	5
North, William, S.F.#	.251	128	415	73	104	1	19	45
Oberkfell, Kenneth, St.L.*	.303	116	422	58	128	3	46	4
Oester, Ronald, Cin.#......	.277	100	303	40	84	2	20	6
Office, Rowland, Mtl.*......	.267	116	292	36	78	6	30	3
Ontiveros, Steven, Chi.#	.208	31	77	7	16	1	3	0
Ott, N. Edward, Pitt.*	.260	120	392	35	102	8	41	1

Batter and Club	AVG	G	AB	R	H	HR	RBI	SB
Parker, David, Pitt.*	.295	139	518	71	153	17	79	10
Parrish, Larry, Mtl.	.254	126	452	55	115	15	72	2
Perkins, Broderick, S.D.*	.370	43	100	18	37	2	14	2
Pettini, Joseph, S.F.	.232	63	190	19	44	1	9	5
Phillips, Michael, St.L.*	.234	63	128	13	30	0	7	0
Pocoroba, Biff, Atl.#	.265	70	83	7	22	2	8	1
Puhl, Terry, Hou.*	.282	141	535	75	151	13	55	27
Pujols, Luis, Hou.	.199	78	221	15	44	0	20	0
Ramirez, Rafael, Atl.	.267	50	165	17	44	2	11	2
Ramsey, Michael, St.L.#	.262	59	126	11	33	0	8	0
Randle, Leonard, Chi.#	.276	130	489	67	135	5	39	19
Reitz, Kenneth, St.L.	.270	151	523	39	141	8	58	0
Reuschel, Ricky, Chi.	.159	44	82	4	13	0	5	0
Reuss, Jerry, L.A.*	.088	37	68	4	6	1	3	0
Reynolds, G. Craig, Hou.*	.226	137	381	34	86	3	28	2
Richards, Eugene, S.D.*	.301	158	642	91	193	4	41	61
Robinson, William, Pitt.	.287	100	272	28	78	12	36	1
Rodriguez, Aurelio, S.D.	.200	89	175	7	35	2	13	1
Rogers, Stephen, Mtl.	.160	38	81	7	13	0	7	0
Rose, Peter, Phil.#	.282	162	655	95	185	1	64	12
Royster, Jeron, Atl.	.242	123	392	42	95	1	20	22
Russell, William, L.A.	.264	130	466	38	123	3	34	13
Ruthven, Richard, Phil.	.235	33	68	7	16	0	8	1
Ryan, L. Nolan, Hou.	.086	35	70	5	6	1	6	0
Sadek, Michael, S.F.	.252	64	151	14	38	1	16	0
Salazar, Luis, S.D.	.337	44	169	28	57	1	25	11
Schmidt, Michael, Phil.	.286	150	548	104	157	48	121	12
Scioscia, Michael, L.A.*	.254	54	134	8	34	1	8	1
Scott, Anthony, St.L.#	.251	143	415	51	104	0	28	22
Scott, Rodney, Mtl.#	.224	154	567	84	127	0	46	63
Simmons, Ted, St.L.#	.303	145	495	84	150	21	98	1
Smith, C. Reginald, L.A.#	.322	92	311	47	100	15	55	5
Smith, Lonnie, Phil.	.339	100	298	69	101	3	20	33
Smith, Osborne, S.D.#	.230	158	609	67	140	0	35	57
Speier, Chris, Mtl.	.265	128	388	35	103	1	32	0
Spilman, W. Harry, Cin.*	.267	65	101	14	27	4	19	0
Stargell, Wilver, Pitt.*	.262	67	202	28	53	11	38	0
Stearns, John, N.Y.	.285	91	319	42	91	0	45	7
Stennett, Renaldo, S.F.	.244	120	397	34	97	2	37	4
Strain, Joseph, S.F.	.286	77	189	26	54	0	16	1

Batter and Club	AVG	G	AB	R	H	HR	RBI	SB
Sularz, Guy, S.F.	.246	25	65	3	16	0	3	1
Taveras, Franklin, N.Y.	.279	141	562	65	157	0	25	32
Templeton, Garry, St.L.#	.319	118	504	83	161	4	43	31
Tenace, F. Gene, S.D.	.222	133	316	46	70	17	50	4
Thomas, Derrel, L.A.#	.266	117	297	32	79	1	22	7
Thomasson, Gary, L.A.*	.216	80	111	6	24	1	12	0
Thompson, V. Scot, Chi.*	.212	102	226	26	48	2	13	6
Tracy, James, Chi.*	.254	42	122	12	31	3	9	2
Trevino, Alejandro, N.Y.	.256	106	355	26	91	0	37	0
Trillo, J. Manuel, Phil.	.292	141	531	68	155	7	43	8
Turner, John, S.D.*	.288	85	153	22	44	3	18	8
Tyson, Michael, Chi.#	.238	123	341	34	81	3	23	1
Unser, Delbert, Phil.*	.264	96	110	15	29	0	10	0
Vail, Michael, Chi.	.298	114	312	30	93	6	47	2
Valentine, Ellis, Mtl.	.315	86	311	40	98	13	67	5
Venable, W. McKinley, S.F.*	.268	64	138	13	37	0	10	8
Vuckovich, Peter, St.L.	.183	32	71	4	13	0	7	1
Walling, Dennis, Hou.*	.299	100	284	30	85	3	29	4
Washington, Claudell, N.Y.*	.275	79	284	38	78	10	42	17
Welch, Robert, L.A.	.243	34	70	1	17	0	3	0
White, Jerome, Mtl.#	.262	110	214	22	56	7	23	8
Whitfield, Terry, S.F.*	.296	118	321	38	95	4	26	4
Whitson, Eddie, S.F.	.091	34	66	2	6	0	4	0
Winfield, David, S.D.	.276	162	558	89	154	20	87	23
Wohlford, James, S.F.	.280	91	193	17	54	1	24	1
Yeager, Stephen, L.A.	.211	96	227	20	48	2	20	2
Youngblood, Joel, N.Y.	.276	146	514	58	142	8	69	14

NATIONAL LEAGUE

Pitching

(90 or more innings)
*Pitches Left-handed

*Throws Lefthanded

Pitcher & Club	ERA	W	L	G	IP	H	BB	SO
Alexander, Doyle, Atl.	4.19	14	11	35	232	227	74	114

Pitcher & Club	ERA	W	L	G	IP	H	BB	SO
Allen, Neil, N.Y.	3.71	7	10	59	97	87	40	79
Andujar, Joaquin, Hou. ...	3.91	3	8	35	122	132	43	75
Bahnsen, Stanley, Mtl.	3.07	7	6	57	91	80	33	48
Bibby, James, Pitt.	3.33	19	6	35	238	210	88	144
Blue, Vida, S.F.*	2.97	14	10	31	224	202	61	129
Blyleven, R. Aalbert, Pitt.	3.82	8	13	34	217	219	59	168
Boggs, Thomas, Atl........	3.42	12	9	32	192	180	46	84
Bomback, Mark, N.Y.	4.09	10	8	36	163	191	49	68
Burris, B. Ray, N.Y.........	4.02	7	13	29	170	181	54	83
Camp, Rick, Atl.............	1.92	6	4	77	108	92	29	33
Candelaria, John, Pitt.* ...	4.02	11	14	35	233	246	50	97
Capilla, Douglas, Chi.*	4.10	2	8	39	90	82	51	51
Carlton, Steven, Phil.*.....	2.34	24	9	38	304	243	90	286
Castillo, Robert, L.A.	2.76	8	6	61	98	70	45	60
Caudill, William, Chi.......	2.18	4	6	72	128	100	59	112
Curtis, John, S.D.*	3.51	10	8	30	187	184	67	71
Falcone, Peter, N.Y.*......	4.53	7	10	37	157	163	58	109
Fingers, Roland, S.D.	2.80	11	9	66	103	101	32	69
Forsch, Kenneth, Hou.	3.20	12	13	32	222	230	41	84
Forsch, Robert, St.L.......	3.77	11	10	31	215	225	33	87
Goltz, David, L.A.	4.32	7	11	35	171	198	59	91
Griffin, Thomas, S.F.	2.75	5	1	42	108	80	49	79
Gullickson, William, Mtl...	3.00	10	5	24	141	127	50	120
Hausman, Thomas, N.Y.	3.98	6	5	55	122	125	26	53
Hernandez, Guillermo, Chi.*........................	4.42	1	9	53	108	115	45	75
Hooton, Burt, L.A.	3.65	14	8	34	207	194	64	118
Hume, Thomas, Cin.	2.56	9	10	78	137	121	38	68
Jones, Randall, S.D.*	3.92	5	13	24	154	165	29	53
Kaat, James, St.L.*........	3.81	8	7	49	130	140	33	36
Knepper, Robert, S.F.*....	4.10	9	16	35	215	242	61	103
Krukow, Michael, Chi......	4.39	10	15	34	205	200	80	130
LaCoss, Michael, Cin.	4.63	10	12	34	169	207	68	59
Lamp, Dennis, Chi.	5.19	10	14	41	203	259	82	83
Lavelle, Gary, S.F.*........	3.42	6	8	62	100	106	36	66
Lea, Charles, Mtl...........	3.72	7	5	21	104	103	55	56
Lee, William, Mtl.*.........	4.96	4	6	24	118	156	22	34
Leibrandt, Charles, Cin.*..	4.24	10	9	36	174	200	54	62

Pitcher & Club	ERA	W	L	G	IP	H	BB	SO
Lerch, Randy, Phil.*	5.16	4	14	30	150	178	55	57
Lucas, Gary, S.D.*	3.24	5	8	46	150	138	43	85
Martinez, Silvio, St.L.	4.80	5	10	25	120	127	48	39
Matula, Richard, Atl.	4.58	11	13	33	177	195	60	62
McGlothen, Lynn, Chi.	4.80	12	14	39	182	211	64	119
McGraw, Frank, Phil.*	1.47	5	4	57	92	62	23	75
McWilliams, Larry, Atl.*	4.94	9	14	30	164	188	39	77
Minton, Gregory, S.F.	2.47	4	6	68	91	81	34	42
Montefusco, John, S.F.	4.38	4	8	22	113	120	39	85
Moskau, Paul, Cin.	4.00	9	7	33	153	147	41	94
Mura, Stephen, S.D.	3.67	8	7	37	169	149	86	109
Niekro, Joseph, Hou.	3.55	20	12	37	256	268	79	127
Niekro, Philip, Atl.	3.63	15	18	40	275	256	85	176
Norman, Fredie, Mtl.*	4.13	4	4	48	98	96	40	58
Palmer, David, Mtl.	2.98	8	6	24	130	124	30	73
Pastore, Frank, Cin.	3.26	13	7	27	185	161	42	110
Price, Joseph, Cin.*	3.57	7	3	24	111	95	37	44
Rasmussen, Eric, S.D.	4.38	4	11	40	111	130	33	50
Reardon, Jeffrey, N.Y.	2.62	8	7	61	110	96	47	101
Reed, Ronald, Phil.	4.05	7	5	55	91	88	30	54
Reuschel, Ricky, Chi.	3.40	11	13	38	257	281	76	140
Reuss, Jerry, L.A.*	2.52	18	6	37	229	193	40	111
Rhoden, Richard, Pitt.	3.83	7	5	20	127	133	40	70
Richard, James, Hou.	1.89	10	4	17	114	65	40	119
Ripley, Allen, S.F.	4.14	9	10	23	113	119	36	65
Robinson, Don, Pitt.	3.99	7	10	29	160	157	45	103
Rogers, Stephen, Mtl.	2.98	16	11	37	281	247	85	147
Romo, Enrique, Pitt.	3.27	5	5	74	124	117	28	82
Ruhle, Vernon, Hou.	2.38	12	4	28	159	148	29	55
Ruthven, Richard, Phil.	3.55	17	10	33	223	241	74	86
Ryan, L. Nolan, Hou.	3.35	11	10	35	234	205	98	200
Sambito, Joseph, Hou.*	2.20	8	4	64	90	65	22	75
Sanderson, Scott, Mtl.	3.11	16	11	33	211	206	56	125
Seaver, G. Thomas, Cin.	3.64	10	8	26	168	140	59	101
Shirley, Robert, S.D.*	3.55	11	12	59	137	143	54	67
Smith, David, Hou.	1.92	7	5	57	103	90	32	85
Solomon, Eddie, Pitt.	2.70	7	3	26	100	96	37	35
Sosa, Elias, Mtl.	3.06	9	6	67	94	104	19	58

Pitcher & Club	ERA	W	L	G	IP	H	BB	SO
Soto, Mario, Cin............	3.08	10	8	53	190	126	84	182
Sutcliffe, Richard, L.A.....	5.56	3	9	42	110	122	55	59
Sutter, H. Bruce, Chi......	2.65	5	8	60	102	90	34	76
Sutton, Donald, L.A.	2.21	13	5	32	212	163	47	128
Swan, Craig, N.Y...........	3.59	5	9	21	128	117	30	79
Sykes, Robert, St.L.*......	4.64	6	10	27	126	134	54	50
Tekulve, Kenton, Pitt.	3.39	8	12	78	93	96	40	47
Tidrow, Richard, Chi.......	2.79	6	5	84	116	97	53	97
Vuckovich, Peter, St.L. ...	3.41	12	9	32	222	203	68	132
Walk, Robert, Phil.	4.56	11	7	27	152	163	71	94
Welch, Robert, L.A.	3.28	14	9	32	214	190	79	141
Whitson, Eddie, S.F.	3.10	11	13	34	212	222	56	90
Wise, Richard, S.D.	3.68	6	8	27	154	172	37	59
Zachry, Patrick, N.Y.......	3.00	6	10	28	165	145	58	88

LATE NEWS

Kansas City signed free-agent 1B Lee May.

Houston signed free-agent C-IF Dave Roberts.

California signed free-agent P John D'Acquisto.

Chicago Cubs sent OF Jerry Martin and OF Jesus Figueroa to San Francisco for P Phil Nastu and IF Joe Strain, then traded OF Mike Vail to Cincinnati for OF Hector Cruz.

Oakland traded SS Mario Guerrero to Seattle.

Chicago White Sox dealt P Rich Wortham to Montreal for IF Tony Bernazard.

Detroit traded OF Dave Stegman to San Diego for P Dennis Kinney.

New York Mets sent P Roy Lee Jackson to Toronto for IF-OF Bob Bailor, signed free-agents 1B-OF Rusty Staub and IF Mike Cubbage, and traded P John Pacella and IF Jose Moreno to San Diego for P Randy Jones.